IAN R. MITCHELL was born in Aberdeen, spe[...]
Torry and Kincorth. He graduated in History [...]
in 1973, after a couple of drop-out years working as a paper mill
labourer and engineering machinist, and subsequently moved to
Glasgow. Ian taught History at Clydebank College for over 20 years and
whilst there wrote a standard textbook on *Bismarck and the Development of Germany.* He has written several books on mountaineering
including *Mountain Days and Bothy Nights* (1987), and *A View from the
Ridge* (both co-written with Dave Brown), which won the Boardman-
Tasker Prize for Mountain Literature in 1991. More recently he has
developed an interest in urban heritage and walking, which led to *This
City Now: Glasgow and its Working Class Past* (2005), the prototype
for *Clydeside: Red, Orange and Green.*

Other works by Ian R. Mitchell published by Luath Press

Non-Fiction

Mountain Days and Bothy Nights (1987) with Dave Brown
A View from the Ridge (1991, re-issued 2007) also with Dave Brown
Scotland's Mountains before the Mountaineers (1998)
On the Trail of Queen Victoria in the Highlands (2001)
Walking through Scotland's History (2000, re-issued 2007)
This City Now: Glasgow and its Working Class Past (2005)

Fiction

Mountain Outlaw: Ewan MacPhee (2003)
Winter in Berlin, or The Mitropa Smile (2009)

Clydeside:
Red, Orange and Green

IAN R. MITCHELL

Luath Press Limited

EDINBURGH

www.luath.co.uk

First published 2010

ISBN: 978-1-906307-70-7

The publishers acknowledge the support of

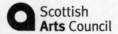
Scottish
Arts Council

towards the publication of this volume.

The paper used in this book is recyclable. It is elemental chlorine free
(ECF) and manufactured from sustainable wood pulp forests, This paper
and its manufacture are approved by the National Association of Paper
Merchants (NAPM), working towards a more sustainable future.

Printed and bound by
Thomson Litho, East Kilbride

Typeset in 11 point Sabon
by 3btype.com

Contents

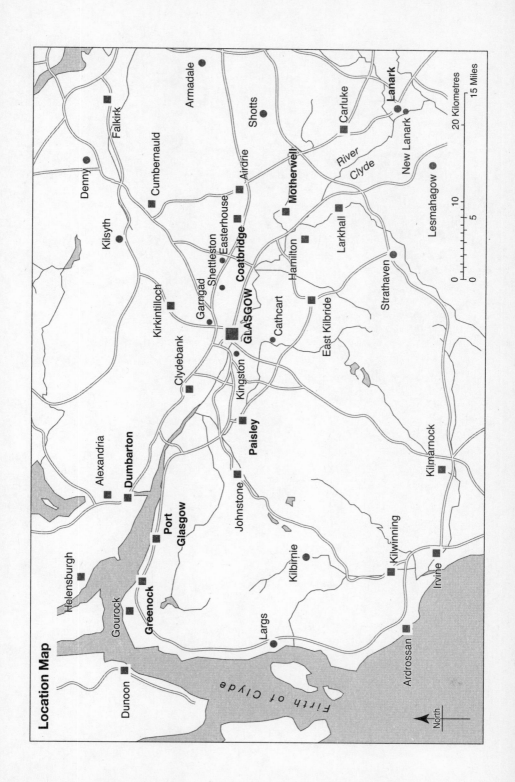

Location Map

Dunoon · Helensburgh · Gourock · **Greenock** · **Port Glasgow** · Alexandria · **Dumbarton** · Denny · Falkirk · Armadale · Kilsyth · Cumbernauld · Shotts · Kirkintilloch · Garngad · Shettleston · Easterhouse · Airdrie · Carluke · **Lanark** · New Lanark · Clydebank · **GLASGOW** · **Coatbridge** · **Motherwell** · Kingston · Cathcart · Hamilton · Larkhall · River Clyde · Paisley · East Kilbride · Strathaven · Lesmahagow · Johnstone · Kilbirnie · Kilwinning · Kilmarnock · Largs · Irvine · Ardrossan

Firth of Clyde

North

0 5 10
0 20 Kilometres
15 Miles

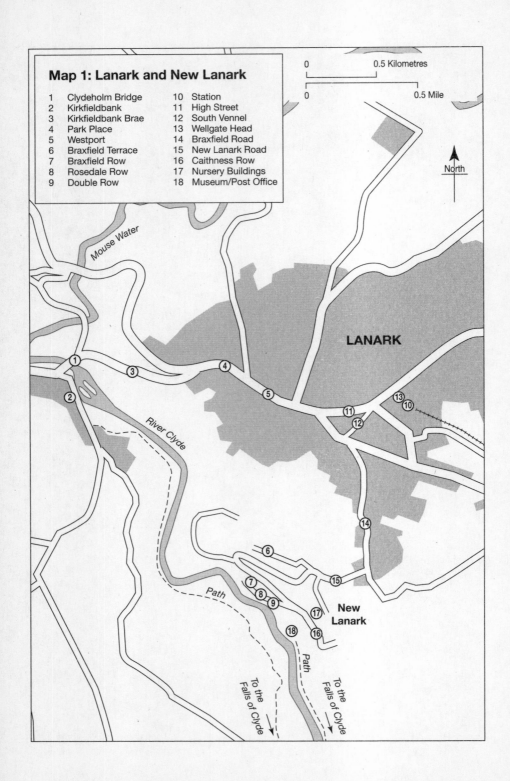

Map 1: Lanark and New Lanark

1   Clydeholm Bridge
2   Kirkfieldbank
3   Kirkfieldbank Brae
4   Park Place
5   Westport
6   Braxfield Terrace
7   Braxfield Row
8   Rosedale Row
9   Double Row
10 Station
11 High Street
12 South Vennel
13 Wellgate Head
14 Braxfield Road
15 New Lanark Road
16 Caithness Row
17 Nursery Buildings
18 Museum/Post Office

0   0.5 Kilometres

0   0.5 Mile

North

Mouse Water

LANARK

River Clyde

Path

New
Lanark

To the
Falls of Clyde

To the
Falls of Clyde

Path

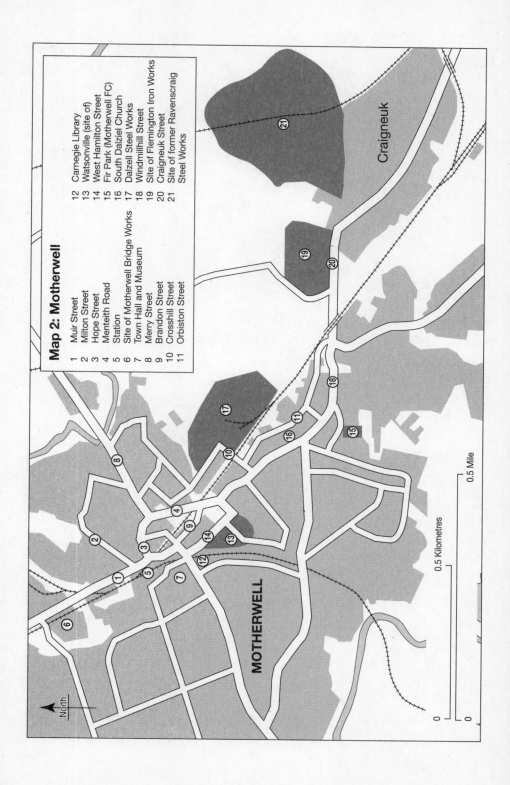

Map 2: Motherwell

1 Muir Street
2 Milton Street
3 Hope Street
4 Menteith Road
5 Station
6 Site of Motherwell Bridge Works
7 Town Hall and Museum
8 Merry Street
9 Brandon Street
10 Crosshill Street
11 Orbiston Street
12 Carnegie Library
13 Watsonville (site of)
14 West Hamilton Street
15 Fir Park (Motherwell FC)
16 South Dalziel Church
17 Dalzell Steel Works
18 Windmillhill Street
19 Site of Flemington Iron Works
20 Craigneuk Street
21 Site of former Ravenscraig
   Steel Works

MOTHERWELL

Craigneuk

North

0.5 Kilometres

0.5 Mile

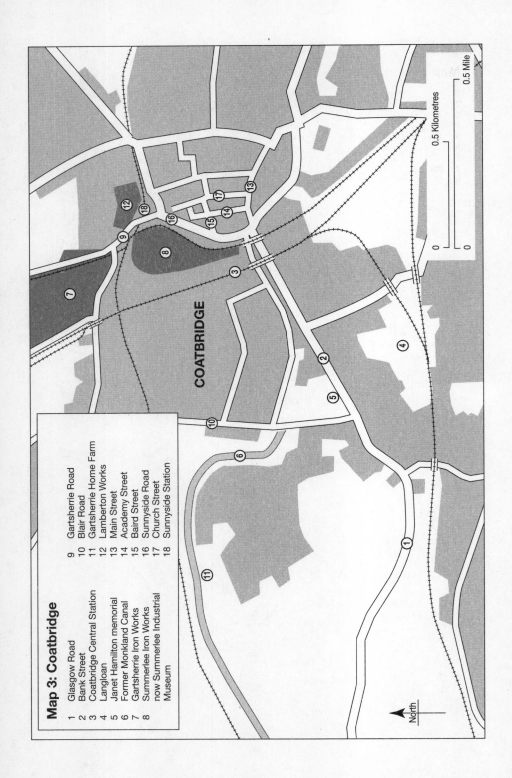

Map 3: Coatbridge

1 Glasgow Road
2 Bank Street
3 Coatbridge Central Station
4 Langloan
5 Janet Hamilton memorial
6 Former Monkland Canal
7 Gartsherrie Iron Works
8 Summerlee Iron Works
  now Summerlee Industrial
  Museum
9 Gartsherrie Road
10 Blair Road
11 Gartsherrie Home Farm
12 Lamberton Works
13 Main Street
14 Academy Street
15 Baird Street
16 Sunnyside Road
17 Church Street
18 Sunnyside Station

COATBRIDGE

North

0.5 Kilometres
0.5 Mile

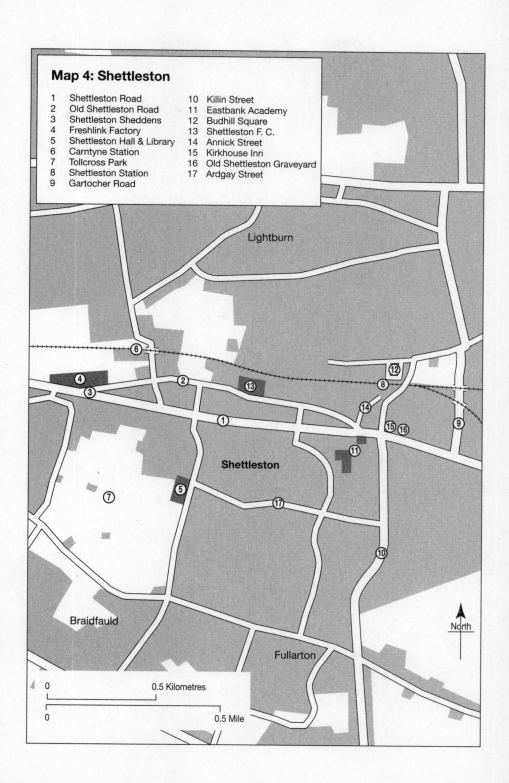

Map 4: Shettleston

1	Shettleston Road	10	Killin Street
2	Old Shettleston Road	11	Eastbank Academy
3	Shettleston Sheddens	12	Budhill Square
4	Freshlink Factory	13	Shettleston F. C.
5	Shettleston Hall & Library	14	Annick Street
6	Carntyne Station	15	Kirkhouse Inn
7	Tollcross Park	16	Old Shettleston Graveyard
8	Shettleston Station	17	Ardgay Street
9	Gartocher Road		

Lightburn

Shettleston

Braidfauld

Fullarton

North

0   0.5 Kilometres

0   0.5 Mile

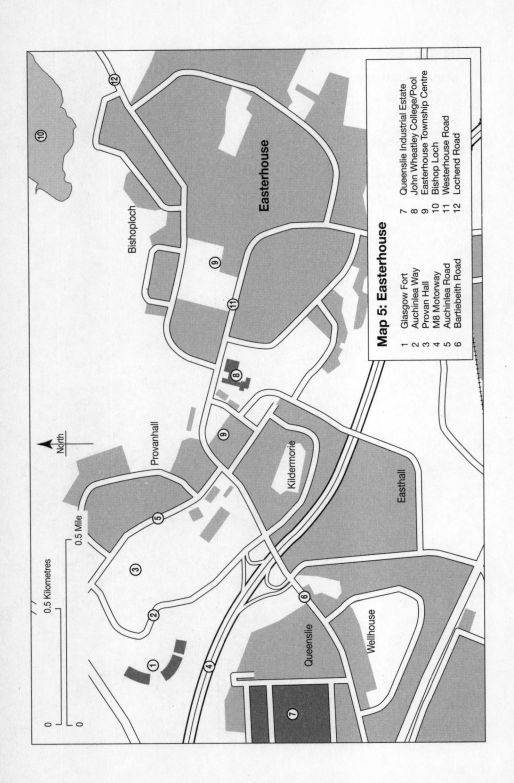

Map 5: Easterhouse

1 Glasgow Fort
2 Auchinlea Way
3 Provan Hall
4 M8 Motorway
5 Auchinlea Road
6 Bartiebeith Road
7 Queenslie Industrial Estate
8 John Wheatley College/Pool
9 Easterhouse Township Centre
10 Bishop Loch
11 Westerhouse Road
12 Lochend Road

Bishoploch

Easterhouse

Provanhall

Kildermorie

Easthall

Queenslie

Wellhouse

North

0.5 Kilometres

0.5 Mile

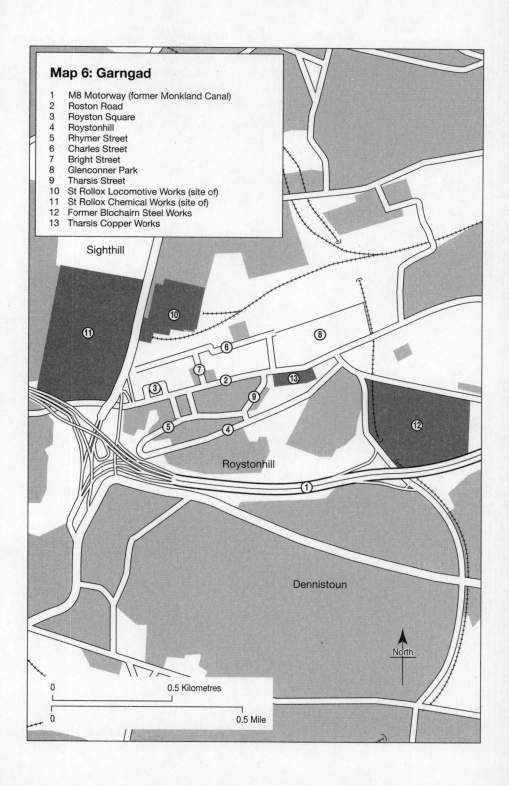

Map 6: Garngad

1. M8 Motorway (former Monkland Canal)
2. Roston Road
3. Royston Square
4. Roystonhill
5. Rhymer Street
6. Charles Street
7. Bright Street
8. Glenconner Park
9. Tharsis Street
10. St Rollox Locomotive Works (site of)
11. St Rollox Chemical Works (site of)
12. Former Blochairn Steel Works
13. Tharsis Copper Works

Sighthill

Roystonhill

Dennistoun

North

0   0.5 Kilometres

0   0.5 Mile

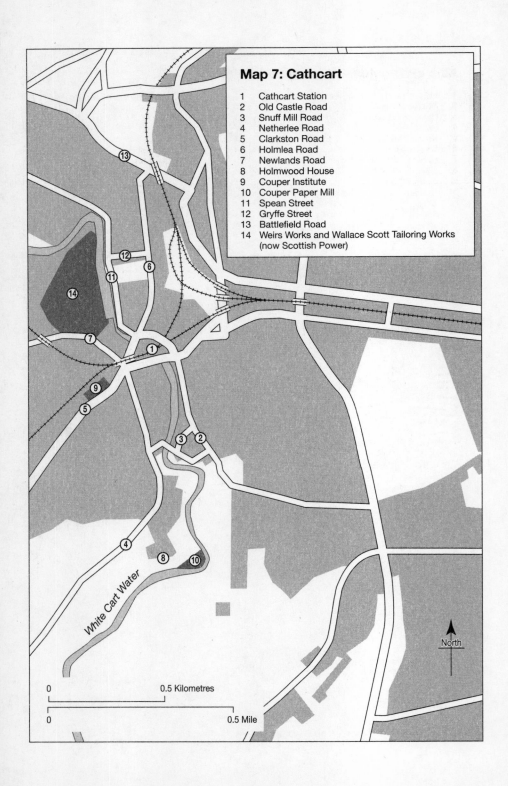

Map 7: Cathcart

1 Cathcart Station
2 Old Castle Road
3 Snuff Mill Road
4 Netherlee Road
5 Clarkston Road
6 Holmlea Road
7 Newlands Road
8 Holmwood House
9 Couper Institute
10 Couper Paper Mill
11 Spean Street
12 Gryffe Street
13 Battlefield Road
14 Weirs Works and Wallace Scott Tailoring Works
  (now Scottish Power)

White Cart Water

0   0.5 Kilometres

0   0.5 Mile

North

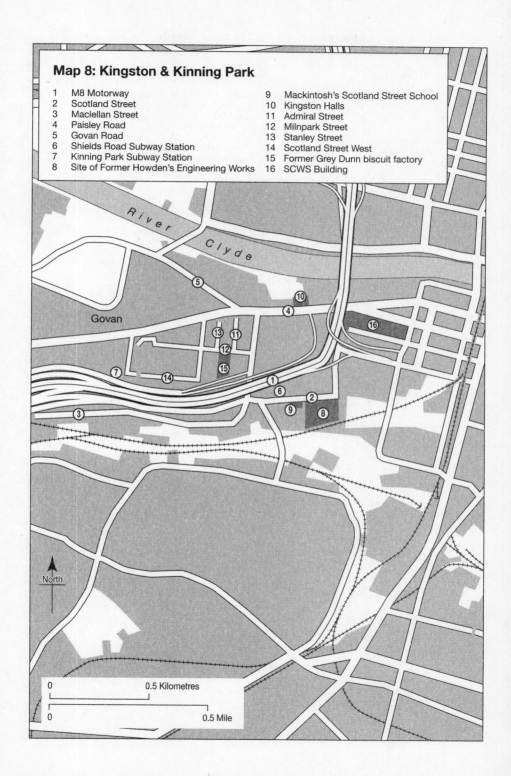

Map 8: Kingston & Kinning Park

1 M8 Motorway
2 Scotland Street
3 Maclellan Street
4 Paisley Road
5 Govan Road
6 Shields Road Subway Station
7 Kinning Park Subway Station
8 Site of Former Howden's Engineering Works

9 Mackintosh's Scotland Street School
10 Kingston Halls
11 Admiral Street
12 Milnpark Street
13 Stanley Street
14 Scotland Street West
15 Former Grey Dunn biscuit factory
16 SCWS Building

River Clyde

Govan

North

0   0.5 Kilometres

0   0.5 Mile

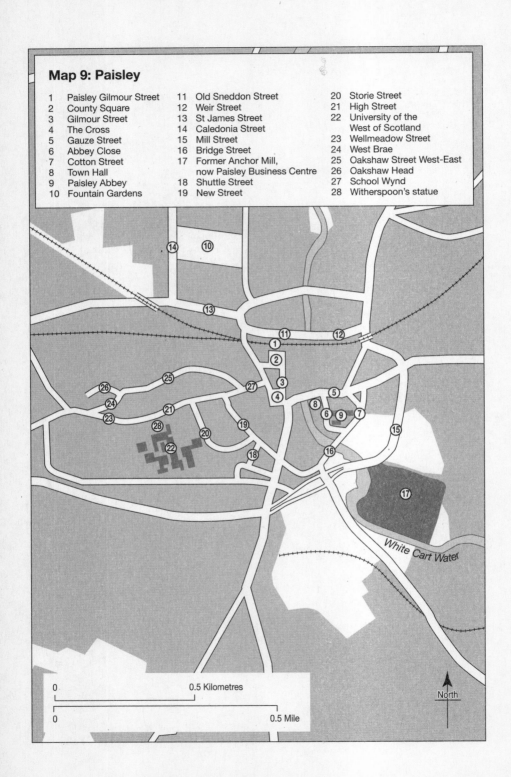

Map 9: Paisley

1 Paisley Gilmour Street
2 County Square
3 Gilmour Street
4 The Cross
5 Gauze Street
6 Abbey Close
7 Cotton Street
8 Town Hall
9 Paisley Abbey
10 Fountain Gardens

11 Old Sneddon Street
12 Weir Street
13 St James Street
14 Caledonia Street
15 Mill Street
16 Bridge Street
17 Former Anchor Mill,
   now Paisley Business Centre
18 Shuttle Street
19 New Street

20 Storie Street
21 High Street
22 University of the
   West of Scotland
23 Wellmeadow Street
24 West Brae
25 Oakshaw Street West-East
26 Oakshaw Head
27 School Wynd
28 Witherspoon's statue

White Cart Water

0   0.5 Kilometres
0   0.5 Mile

North

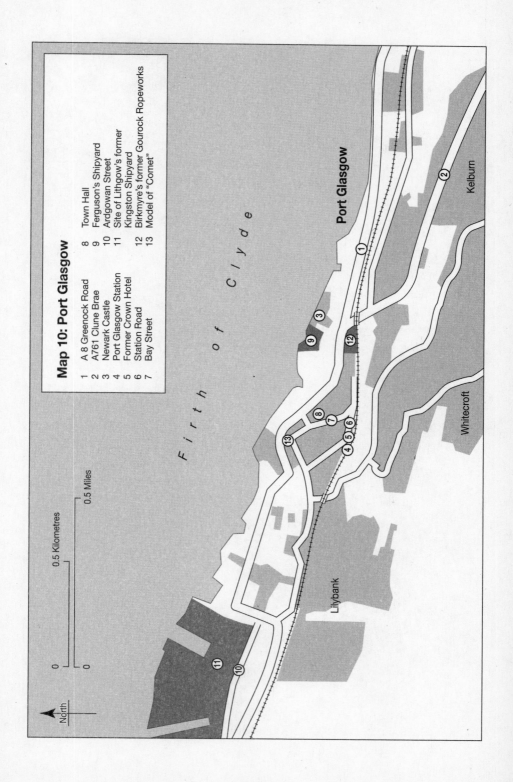

Map 10: Port Glasgow

1 A 8 Greenock Road
2 A761 Clune Brae
3 Newark Castle
4 Port Glasgow Station
5 Former Crown Hotel
6 Station Road
7 Bay Street

8 Town Hall
9 Ferguson's Shipyard
10 Ardgowan Street
11 Site of Lithgow's former
   Kingston Shipyard
12 Birkmyre's former Gourock Ropeworks
13 Model of "Comet"

0.5 Kilometres
0.5 Miles

North

Firth of Clyde

Port Glasgow

Kelburn

Whitecroft

Lilybank

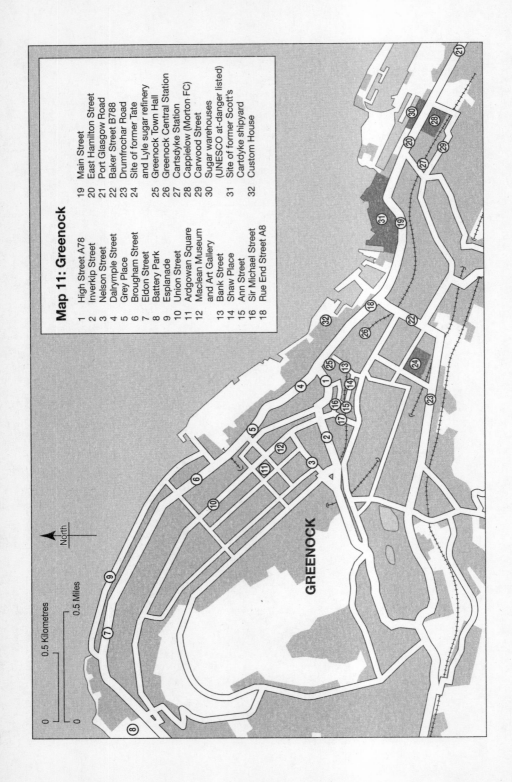

Map 11: Greenock

1	High Street A78
2	Inverkip Street
3	Nelson Street
4	Dalrymple Street
5	Grey Place
6	Brougham Street
7	Eldon Street
8	Battery Park
9	Esplanade
10	Union Street
11	Ardgowan Square
12	Maclean Museum and Art Gallery
13	Bank Street
14	Shaw Place
15	Ann Street
16	Sir Michael Street
18	Rue End Street A8
19	Main Street
20	East Hamilton Street
21	Port Glasgow Road
22	Baker Street B788
23	Drumfrochar Road
24	Site of former Tate and Lyle sugar refinery
25	Greenock Town Hall
26	Greenock Central Station
27	Cartsdyke Station
28	Cappielow (Morton FC)
29	Carwood Street
30	Sugar warehouses (UNESCO at-danger listed)
31	Site of former Scott's Cartdyke shipyard
32	Custom House

North

0.5 Kilometres
0.5 Miles

GREENOCK

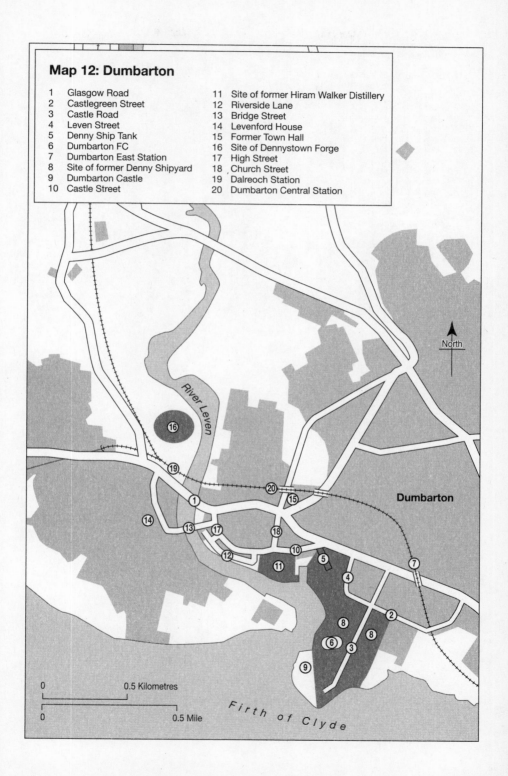

Map 12: Dumbarton

1 Glasgow Road
2 Castlegreen Street
3 Castle Road
4 Leven Street
5 Denny Ship Tank
6 Dumbarton FC
7 Dumbarton East Station
8 Site of former Denny Shipyard
9 Dumbarton Castle
10 Castle Street
11 Site of former Hiram Walker Distillery
12 Riverside Lane
13 Bridge Street
14 Levenford House
15 Former Town Hall
16 Site of Dennystown Forge
17 High Street
18 Church Street
19 Dalreoch Station
20 Dumbarton Central Station

North

River Leven

Dumbarton

Firth of Clyde

0   0.5 Kilometres

0   0.5 Mile

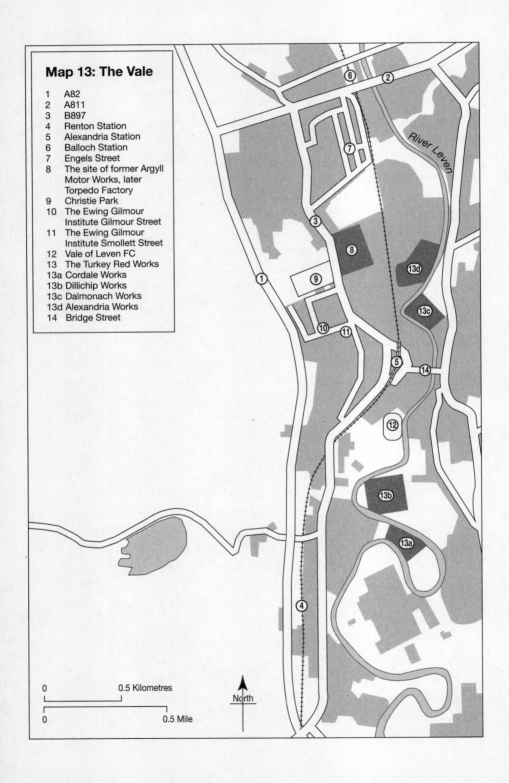

Map 13: The Vale

1 A82
2 A811
3 B897
4 Renton Station
5 Alexandria Station
6 Balloch Station
7 Engels Street
8 The site of former Argyll Motor Works, later Torpedo Factory
9 Christie Park
10 The Ewing Gilmour Institute Gilmour Street
11 The Ewing Gilmour Institute Smollett Street
12 Vale of Leven FC
13 The Turkey Red Works
13a Cordale Works
13b Dillichip Works
13c Dalmonach Works
13d Alexandria Works
14 Bridge Street

River Leven

0   0.5 Kilometres

0   0.5 Mile

North

Foreword

IN THE PREFACE to the first German edition of his seminal study *The Condition of the Working Class in England*, Friedrich Engels bemoans the paucity of studies of the conditions in which ordinary working people live and work. We have, of course, come a long way since Engels penned those comments in 1845, but it still seems fair to complain that the majority of books on Glasgow and the West of Scotland fail to give due heed to the working-class past that shapes their social – and physical – geography. Ian R. Mitchell's excellent volume, *This City Now: Glasgow and its Working Class Past* (Luath Press, 2005), did much to address this complaint, and in his present book, *Clydeside: Red, Orange and Green*, Ian now broadens his canvas by looking at other working-class districts in Glasgow and by stepping further afield to take in neighbouring areas along the banks of the River Clyde.

Like its predecessor, *Clydeside* is a revelation, and will provide much stimulus for those who believe that they already know Clydeside well to get on their walking shoes and really get to know it better. I myself was born in Dumbarton, and spent the first 22 years of my life in Clydebank and Glasgow. I thought I knew the city and its environs well, but although I have heard of all 13 areas covered in this book, I have in fact only very briefly visited Dumbarton, Greenock and Paisley. Thanks to Ian's work, I now have good reason to return to those areas, and to make maiden visits to the others, well equipped by *Clydeside* to appreciate their history and social geography from the viewpoint of the working people who made – and make – them what they are.

I think that Ian's remarks on the Scottish Socialist Party (SSP) in Chapter 8 are somewhat harsh. Far from being politically ineffective in the Holyrood Parliament between 2003 and 2007, the SSP exerted genuine political pressure on the (then) Labour Executive – forcing them, for example, to make concessions on prescription charges in the NHS in Scotland.

From Robert Owen's utopian socialist project in New Lanark to Engels Street in Balloch on the shores of Loch Lomond, Ian is an affable and entertaining guide with an eye for the street theatre and an ear for the banter – and, most importantly of all, a deep empathy with the working-class inhabitants, both past and present, of the areas he covers. Whether you are a newcomer, a long-standing resident, or an ex-pat, Ian R. Mitchell's *Clydeside* will give you insight, enlightenment and pleasure.

Alex Miller
Professor of Philosophy
University of Birmingham

Introduction

A River Runs Through It

CLYDESIDE. What does the word evoke?

Despite the fact that the River Clyde runs though a hundred miles of what is some of the loveliest and most historically rich countryside in Scotland, the term Clydeside does not convey images of the Falls of Clyde, Bothwell Castle and Dun Breatainn to most.

Instead, it conveys images of heavy industry, of coal mines and steel works and shipyards and engineering, and it conveys images of technological innovation in these fields. It also conjures up images of human suffering, of appalling housing and working conditions. It conveys images of struggle, of the birth of the labour movement, of strikes, of political conflict. It conveys in many ways what the word 'Glasgow' does itself, but on a larger geographical canvas.

The publication of my book on Glasgow's working-class past, *This City Now*, was greeted with reviews that were encouragingly positive. More important to me, it led to a whole series of outlets in the form of talks that I gave on the book, walks that I conducted based around its chapters, and even to a course taught at Glasgow University's Department of Adult and Continuing Education. Through these activities I met many of the sort of people I had written the book for, and of whom it was about.

A follow-up seemed a fruitful project, and for a while I meditated a second book on Glasgow, having realised that there were several areas I had neglected in *This City Now*, but which nonetheless merited attention. Rather than do this, though, I decided that it would be better to use these new chapters on Glasgow as a link, a halfway house, between other studies that I had been undertaking of various towns on the Lower Clyde, with forays that I had always promised myself into the lesser-known lands of Lanarkshire.

I felt justified in this not only by the fact that the river could give the geographical unity to a collection of separate profiles of Clydeside towns, in a similar way to that which Glasgow itself had given to *This City Now*, but also that economically and culturally, the Clyde composed a unity. Lanark may be (almost) as near to Edinburgh as it is to Glasgow, but the capital could as well be on the moon for Lanark, whilst Glasgow is the sun which holds it in its gravity. Greenock is the same distance from Glasgow as Kilmarnock. Whilst the latter is outwith Glasgow's ambiance, the former is like a satellite of the city.

And yet, despite these similarities, the towns of Clydeside give such an enormous variety of working-class experiences – industrially, in housing, in politics and in other areas, as well as having such varied built environments, and having produced widely differing political figures, that I felt there was no chance of an endless repetition, in any attempt to treat the settlements between Lanark and Greenock as a unity. Clydeside is all the things the name conjures up but much more – as I hope to show, it is a 'River City', joined together by much more than the river running through it.

Most of all, it is welded together by two centuries of working-class history.

CHAPTER I

New Lanark:
A New View of Society

THE RIVER CLYDE rises obscurely in the rounded hills of the Upper Ward
of Lanarkshire, to the south-east of the town of Lanark. Here is a somewhat bleak landscape, of moorland plateau with few trees. Today, this
is a thinly populated region containing a small portion of Lanarkshire's
600,000 people. But in the past it was an area of importance, focused
on the former county town of Lanark, previously the seat of local
administration and justice. Though industrial development was to move
the locus of population, wealth and power up the River Clyde, most
noticeably to Glasgow itself, 35 miles away, events of significance to the
history of the working class were to take place in this peripheral region
– despite the Upper Ward remaining predominantly agricultural. Indeed,
as well as the source of the River Clyde, the region has a claim to being
a source of the idea of socialism itself, through its association with the
life and ideas of Robert Owen and the New Lanark cotton mills. Owen
was the first to coin the term 'socialism', though what was meant by the
word is subject to some dispute.

The Upper Ward was no stranger to rebel-
liousness and heretical ideas. This was one of
the main power bases of the Covenanting
movement in Scotland in the 17th century.
Readers of Walter Scott's *Old Mortality* will
know the story of how the Lanarkshire and
Ayrshire peasantries supplied the bulk of the
supporters of the ill-fated rebellion of 1685,
which started victoriously at the battle of
Drumclog near Lanark, and ended disastrously
at Bothwell Brig.

Craignethan Castle, which lies in Upper
Clydesdale, features in Scott's great novel as

ROBERT OWEN c.1800
A man sure of himself

'Tillietudlem'. And in 1688–9 the Upper Ward was to provide the recruitment base for the Cameronian forces that defeated the first Jacobite rebellion at the Battle of Dunkeld. Even further back, in 1297, it was in Lanark that William Wallace was reputed to have raised the standard of rebellion against English rule.

At the time of the Radical War of 1820, the town of Strathaven, near Lanark, provided an early working-class martyr in James Wilson, executed in Glasgow for treason at the age of 60. Twenty-thousand people watched his funeral, in sympathy rather than vengeance, and cries of 'Shame!' greeted his execution. Wilson was one of the leaders of the armed rebellion undertaken in protest against living conditions after the Napoleonic wars and especially against the hated Corn Laws of 1815. He was one of the 600 weavers in Strathaven who were facing increasingly hard times. The aims of the Radicals, in the village and elsewhere, were for political reform and votes for working men. They armed, made bullets and drilled, but were tricked into a premature uprising, 50 of them marching to the Cathkin Braes outside Glasgow, only to find the expected support from elsewhere had not materialised. Dispersal saved the others, but not Wilson.

Robert Owen's socialism

Robert Owen probably knew nothing about the Covenanters and their local traditions. If he had, he would doubtless have seen their struggle as an example of the pernicious effects of that religious fanaticism which he resolutely opposed. For Owen was probably the first crusading atheist in the UK, actively opposed to all religions and their works. Though he did not comment on the Radical War, or on James Wilson's fate, Owen was certainly aware of the unrest among the working class after 1815, in Scotland and throughout Britain. He was firmly opposed, however, not only to the idea of taking violent action against political injustice but also to the whole idea of political reform itself, which he saw as a diversion. In his *Address to the Working Classes*, published in 1819, Owen argued that economic and social reform, not political action and change, were the solution to the issues facing them.

Robert Owen was born in Wales in 1771. He was a prodigy, self educating himself to an intellectual atheist position by the age of 10. He entered the developing textile industry and by the time he was 20 he was managing a mill in Manchester. Coming to Glasgow on business, he fell in love with the daughter of David Dale, one of Scotland's leading textile entrepreneurs, and visited the mills that Dale had set up in 1785 with Richard Arkwright at New Lanark. These works utilised the plentiful water below the Falls of Clyde, and employed 1,500 people. In 1799 Owen married Dale's daughter in her father's Glasgow mansion at Charlotte Street, and on 1 January 1800 he took over the management of the New Lanark cotton mills.

Dale was, for that period, quite an enlightened employer, though his many mills prevented close attention to any single one. At New Lanark housing and working conditions were above the (admittedly) awful standards of the time; nevertheless, Dale employed 500 pauper children in the works. He did, however, provide a school and limited social facilities. Owen liked to portray New Lanark as utterly depraved when he first arrived there, though the truth is that his own social experiments built on those of Dale. Initially, Owen was little more than a ruthless, efficient enlightened despot, and there is no suggestion of his later ideas in his early activities.

Owen shortened the working day at New Lanark and reduced the incidence of child labour, as had other employers who had found out that this improved productivity. He overhauled the inefficient company store which sold poor overpriced goods, and by a system of bulk buying and supplying the store from the company's own farms, provided the workers with better and cheaper food. This was so successful that people from Lanark came to shop in the New Lanark store. But this was still a company store, not a co-operative, and the profits were used to offset the costs to Owen and the company of the factory school. Owen also introduced what appears to be an example of village democracy, where neighbourhood 'divisions' within the company's housing chose 'principals', who then selected 12 'jurors' to run communal affairs for a year. However, this was really a conveyor belt for company discipline, ensuring that houses were cleaned and middens removed, that alcohol was not circulating and that the company ethos was imposed – with fines for those who transgressed.

Within the factory rigid discipline was imposed, with wage deductions and dismissal for lateness, pilfering and undue levity. Owen did not invent the 'silent monitor', where a coloured device hung above a person's workplace showing how well they had performed and shaming them if they fell below par, but it was typical of the kind of discipline he enforced. When he wrote his first major work, *A New View of Society*, in 1813, Owen was still no more than an enlightened capitalist, who felt that a patriarchal social discipline was not only good for the workforce but produced higher profits. At this time, the mill paid 12 per cent annually on investments, and by 1813 Owen himself was a millionaire several times over in today's terms. Though social conditions were, in all probability, better at New Lanark than in most, if not all, cotton mills, wages were low – lower than in urban mills in Glasgow, and much lower than in the Lancashire mills. The top-paid male workers earned 10 shillings (50p) a week, and for the females and children it was on a sliding scale downwards from that. Owen was not trusted at all by working-class radicals at this time, and the newspaper *Black Dwarf* criticised his ideas as aiming 'to turn the nation into a workhouse and rear up a community of slaves'.

Following his early conversion to atheism, Owen's second conversion came in the years between 1813 and 1818, during which he met William Godwin many times. Godwin was a reformer whose *Political Justice* is one of the founding texts of anarchist thinking, and under Godwin's influence Owen moved towards the idea of self-governing communities as the solution to the ills of emerging industrial society.

Like Godwin, Owen was a rationalist and believed that ideas were right or wrong and truth could be appreciated by anybody. Thus, while he did propagate to the working classes, he devoted more time and effort spreading his ideas to those with their hands on the levers of power, such as the textile magnate and Tory politician Robert Peel. He expended much energy trying to convince capitalists, politicians and even rulers to adopt his ideas. He visited Aix la Chappelle in 1818 in an attempt to convert the Russian Czar to Owenism, but was

NEW LANARK TICKET FOR WAGES
Allowing workers to purchase cut-price goods at the village store (half a crown

rudely rejected. On this occasion he met the aide of Metternich, another reactionary he hoped to influence, and was told, 'We do not want the masses to become wealthy and independent. How could we govern them if they were?'. Owen was even introduced to Queen Victoria in 1839 by the Prime Minister Lord Melbourne, having been given an opportunity to explain his ideas.

By the early 1820s, Owen had become a socialist. He believed now that the exploitation labour was the source of society's increasing wealth, not 'the productivity of capital', and in his *Report to the County of Lanark* of 1821 (again delivered to an audience of the power-brokers in the county, not the workers) Owen announced his vision of a society based on 'the principle of united labour, expenditure and property, and equal privileges', which he was to increasingly describe as 'socialism'. The tactics to establishing such a society were propaganda and example, not class struggle.

The activities which Owen became involved in were to set up communist colonies, which would be self-sufficient and combine both industrial and agricultural manual labour with intellectual activity. He spent much of his time in the United States, which he saw as more open to his ideas, and much of his money on the New Harmony experiment of 1825–7 in that country. It is not part of our remit here to describe the fate of New Harmony, or of the later attempts at establishing communist colonies that Owen was involved with in England. These failed, partly since the methods Owen had learned in running New Lanark were not the same as those needed for New Harmony. Interestingly, Owen's son, Robert Dale, who was born in Glasgow, stayed in the United States and became a slavery abolitionist, whose pamphlet *The Policy of Emancipation* (1863) greatly influenced Abraham Lincoln.

Enlightenment was Owen's other weapon and he established various organisations, the most influential of which was the Rational Society in the 1840s, which, at its height, had a newspaper with a circulation of 40,000 and organised well-attended meetings at its branches countrywide. One of the audience members at the Rational Society's meetings in Manchester was the young German philosopher Friedrich Engels, who was greatly influenced by Owen some years before he met Marx. But Engels could discern the failings in Owen's approach, which was totally divorced from the class struggle of the workers that Engels saw under his eyes in Manchester, and wrote about in his *Condition of the Working Class in England in 1844*. Engels could also see that Owen's opposition to political reform, including his hostility to the 'rage' of the Chartist movement of the 1840s, turned his group into a sect. Later, Engels was to describe people like Owen in his pamphlet *Socialism: Utopian and Scientific* as those who tried to impose their vision on social reality by example and propaganda, rather than seeing the seeds of social transformation in the struggle taking place before their eyes.

Owen did have an effect on the emerging working-class movement, but it was incidental. While he was in the United States, absent from New Lanark, many people, inspired by his ideas, had set up co-operative stores. The co-operative movement began to spread throughout the UK, but Owen had little real part in the growth of this authentic expression of working-class aspirations. With his hostility to class struggle he was also hostile to strikes, and it is rather surprising that briefly, in 1834, he was involved in the attempt to establish a national trades union movement in the UK, though it is incorrect to see, as many commentators do, the Grand National Consolidated Trades Union (GNCTU), which claimed 500,000 members at its peak, as Owen's creation. But the collapse of the GNCTU, through lock-outs and the victimisation of groups such as the Tolpuddle Martyrs in 1834, ended this brief and exceptional involvement by Owen in real working-class politics.

Meanwhile, what of New Lanark? It would be wrong to suggest that with Owen's conversion to socialism nothing changed at New Lanark. The establishment of the Institute for the Formation of Character in 1816 expanded education, including nursery and primary education, and along the most advanced principles. Physical punishment was banned (as it was in the factory) and children were given dancing and music instruction and a wide variety of interesting lessons. People flocked to New Lanark to view the 'experiment': 2,000 visitors a year from 1815 to 1825, when Owen's involvement ended after a quarter of a century. Most were of the upper and middle classes, and most were tremendously impressed at what they saw. They perceived not only that the workforce was generally well fed and cared for by the standards of the first quarter of the 19th century, but also that here the labouring classes were subject to an enviable degree of social control, which reduced their 'dangerous' tendencies to almost zero. There was no policeman in the village, because there was no crime. One critic, however, was the poet Robert Southey, who observed that Owen 'keeps out of sight from others, and perhaps from himself, that his system, instead of aiming at perfect freedom, can only be kept in play by absolute power'. Even the village shop only became a co-operative store under the control of the inhabitants, after Owen had left New Lanark behind.

For there was no intention of trying (even if his partners would have allowed it) to turn New Lanark into a New Harmony; the workers in the village remained subordinate and low paid. In 1825, frustrated with increasing pressures from his partners and from the local presbytery to include religious education in the school curriculum at New Lanark, and preoccupied with other projects under way across the Atlantic, Owen sold out his share of the works for £40,000 to the Walkers, one of his partners. The Walkers were Quakers and, according to the Factory Inspector of 1833, the mill was still then run 'under the same excellent management and with a view to health, education and general comfort of the workers', as had been the case under Dale and Owen. But the Walkers ran down the mill, and had not even installed ancillary steam power until 1873, which meant the mill was frequently under-powered.

By 1833, the mill employed only 1,000 workers as the Scottish textile industry began to contract under Lancashire competition. Robert Owen had left cotton production at a good time. New Lanark's population had peaked at 2,300 in 1821, and had fallen to 700 by 1891, many of whom did not work in the mill itself. By the latter date, the factory was owned by the Birkmyres of the Gourock Rope Company and had survived by specialising in net and heavy sailcloth manufacture. The works continued to employ about 300 people until it was finally closed in 1968. It was in the wrong place, under-capitalised and unprofitable. The Gourock Rope Company was also unable to financially entertain the prospect of maintaining the social fabric of the village, much of which was unoccupied, as its international importance became more and more recognised. Indeed, the transformation of the mill and factory workers' housing, with the ancillary buildings, into a UNESCO World Heritage Site, took 20 years and the expenditure of well over £10 million. When visiting, it is worth remembering that, whilst Owen does have a claim to be one of the founding fathers of socialism, New Lanark itself was in no way an experiment in support of that idea.

Lanark today

Lanark as a town has suffered from a deficiency of admirers. In the 1720s Daniel Defoe described it as 'but a very indifferent place', and a century later the ever-critical Dorothy Wordsworth commented, 'the doors and windows are dirty, the shops dull' though she thought the marketplace 'decent'. I like Lanark, though it lacks the picturesque affluence of the other Upper Ward towns such as Strathaven and Biggar, and rather exudes something of the demotic grubbiness of Clydeside generally.

Exiting from the station, on the right the way will take you to Lanark's impressive market stance, where 10 fairs a year were held in the 1790s. Today, the Lanimer Fair still takes place in early June, and the Whuppity Scourie on 1 March. Here, too, is a fine statue of William Wallace at the Parish Kirk of St Nicholas, recalling the role of the town as the cradle of his rebellion. The traditional village is well worth a visit and a stroll, but New Lanark lies in the other direction.

The way to 'Owenville' from Lanark station (it is all well signposted) follows South Vennel, and then Wellgatehead, before dropping down Braxfield Road to a set of gatehouses. From there it is a toddle downhill along New Lanark Road to the mill and village, fine views of which appear before it is reached. It is a stunning sight, in its stark simplicity, especially if the sun is shining on the light sandstone. It is not my place here to give a guide to the UNESCO site; the visitor should simply make his or her way around the village, allowing a few hours for the experience. One of the mills has been converted into a hotel, whilst some of the former workers' rows have become a youth hostel. Many of the other houses have been restored and amalgamated as dwellings for residents and commuters, but a central block contains a fine series of examples of workers' housing from the time of Owen through to the 1950s. As you visit the earlier examples, it is worth noting that Owen's provision in terms of housing was little more generous than that of the other capitalists of his period. Sanitation was inadequate, and outbreaks of typhus took place here, as well as cholera, under Owen's rule.

Two villas stand outside the mill, one Dale's house and one Owen's. Again, though this was only an occasional residence for Owen, it is a world apart from the conditions in which the workers lived. As I said previously, New Lanark was not New Harmony, nor did it ever intend to be. A visit to the mill buildings, where some machinery has been restored, gives an example of working conditions 200 years ago. But the jewel in the crown of any visit must be the Institute for the Formation of Character itself, an institution a century or more ahead of its time. Despite some (nowadays alas inevitable) heritage tackiness, a visit to New Lanark is a very valuable experience, though some may feel that Owen's saintliness is overplayed and his failings minimised in the picture of the history here presented.

People came here to see New Lanark in their thousands, but they also came to see the marvellous Falls of Clyde, and so should any visitor today. You leave the mills by following the path alongside the mill lade, which provided water for its huge cast iron mill wheels, and come to a gate beside the small power station, which supplied steam power from the 1870s. An excellent path then goes along the banks of the Clyde past Bonnington Power Station, the construction of which in the 1920s sadly reduced the fall of water on this part of the river, though on certain days the full force is allowed through. Beyond the station, amid scenery of great beauty, is Corra Linn, the largest of the falls, and here we are following in the steps of Wordsworth, Turner, Burns and many others. From here, most retrace their path, but carrying on another half-mile or so is visually rewarding and leads to Bonnington Linn, where a bridge crosses the Clyde. It is now possible to follow a path on the west side of the river, past the ruins of Corra Castle, and from here you get the best views of New Lanark itself. Carrying on downstream, you come to a view of Braxfield Park, where stood the main residence occupied by Owen and his family during his New Lanark years. This mansion was rented from the McQueen family, whose most famous member was the infamous Lord Braxfield, the 'hanging judge' in the trials of many Radicals in the 1790s, including those of Muir and Palmer, whom he sentenced to transportation. The path then goes on to Kirkfieldbank and the Clydeholm Bridge, dating from the 1690s, and from there it is 'a lang pech up the brae' back to Lanark village, and then to the station.

New Lanark was always an exception in the Upper Ward, the only large-scale industrial enterprise in an agricultural region that was initially dominated by fruit-farming dependent on migrant Irish labour, and now-adays is focused on garden centres relying on Polish immigrants. And New Lanark is also exceptional in British industrial and social history as a unique laboratory of social ideas from the early period of the Industrial Revolution.

CHAPTER 2

Motherwell:
Bibliopolis, Steelopolis

COMMUNISM CAME TWICE to Motherwell. In 1825 – led by Abram Coke, with the support of a local radical landowner, Archibald Hamilton – the co-operative living and working settlement known as Orbiston was established. Inspired by the ideas of Robert Owen and aiming at self-sufficiency and equality, the experiment at Orbiston lasted two years before breaking up after Coke's death. Just under a century later, Motherwell created a national sensation by electing Britain's first Communist MP, Walton Newbold, and in Moscow Lenin declared, somewhat optimistically, that 'The steel town Motherwell has been won for communism'.

In 1825, Motherwell was not yet Steelopolis. Indeed, it hardly existed, apart from scattered settlements along the old Roman road. The minister of Dalziel Parish declared in the 1790s: 'In two places only, there are clusters [of houses] together which may be called villages, there being 15 houses in one and 12 in the other' (*Old Statistical Account*). Even when the railway came to the area in the 1830s, things were slow to change, and by 1851 the population was only 2,000, comprising mainly miners who worked in the surrounding collieries. The demand for coal continued to increase and by the First World War there were almost 5,000 miners in the pits surrounding Motherwell. There were 35,000 miners in total in the Lanarkshire coalfield, the principal coalfield in Scotland at this time.

But Motherwell's real growth came with the arrival of the iron and (especially) steel industries. The Motherwell Malleable Iron Works was set up in 1861 with 800 workers, many of them immigrants from Staffordshire in England. Other iron works followed, including that established by David Colville in 1870. At the Dalzell Works, Colville quickly introduced steel production, installing a Siemens open hearth furnace in 1880, and soon the firm became the largest producer of steel in Scotland, eventually owning most of the Scottish steel industry by the

1920s. Iron was largely used in construction work, for example for bridges (Colville's supplied the iron for the rebuilt Tay Bridge in 1879), and steel was supplied for the booming Clyde shipyards. There were almost 6,000 iron- and steel-workers in Motherwell at the start of the 20th century – of whom Colville employed around half.

The railway had made Motherwell, (outside of Glasgow) Scotland's main railway junction, where the Caledonian Railway Company owned workshops as well as stations. In 1911, 1,000 people worked on the railways in Motherwell. Other heavy engineering works followed; the Motherwell Bridge and Engineering Company became leading construction engineers from 1898, and the next year Anderson Boyes was set up to manufacture coal-cutting equipment. This firm was a field leader from the outset, pioneering electrically driven machinery. By 1911, Motherwell was an industrial metropolis of 40,000 people, with a labour force of 13,000 people; 10,000 (almost 80 per cent) of whom worked in heavy industry.

Motherwell was slow to achieve burgh status, partly because the local capitalists and landowners feared being assessed for rates, but it was finally given this in 1875. Even then the local councillors, representing the middle-class ratepayers, were parsimonious in extreme. A town hall was only built in the 1880s when it was underwritten by the Colvilles and Motherwell did not even have a secondary school until 1898. These skinflint capitalists contributed little to charitable works, aside from religious ones. The coal magnate John Watson gave a clock to the parish church, and Colville's a park to the town, and that was about it. This Gradgrind-like mentality was in stark contrast to the enormous social needs faced by Motherwell. Glasgow, not to mention Govan or Paisley, at this time was a recipient of much capitalist philanthropy. Even by Victorian standards, Motherwell was a hard place in which to live. In his excellent book *Steelopolis*, upon which my own account of the town is heavily based, Rob Duncan observes:

Motherwell was a grim and ugly place for the majority of its people... workers and their families lived among the grime and pollution from hundreds of chimneys belching black smoke, the most unfortunate were those living near the Malleable Iron Works, which emitted black chemical smoke all day.

Pollution increased mortality rates. In Motherwell in 1911, the infant mortality rate was 130 in every 1,000 births. (For comparison, in ship-building Govan it was 85.) In addition, overcrowding in Motherwell, as with all Lanarkshire industrial towns, was much worse than even in Glasgow. In the same year of 1911, in Motherwell 70 per cent of families lived in one- or two-roomed houses; in Glasgow the respective figure was 55 per cent. Part of the problem was that the area was so undermined with colliery workings that very few tenements could be built; instead, miners' rows and two-storey buildings were the norm. The town's bound-aries were constricted, as local landowners and capitalists fought against their extension, meaning that the Motherwell's population doubled in the years between 1892 and 1908 on the same area. Combined with the low wages and poor working conditions which operated in most of the local industries, this was an explosive mixture.

Miners in Lanarkshire were, according to the *North British Daily Mail* in 1869, 'reduced to a condition little better than that of slaves who worked for food and raiment'. In Motherwell's mining satellites such as Watsonville, they paid rent to the company for their tied housing in the squalid miners' rows, and had to buy in the overpriced company stores in a variant of the 'truck' system. They were paid in arrears, usually of a fortnight but sometimes a month, and they were given wage advances at credit. This led to many miners getting into permanent debt with the coal companies. There were wage deductions for the company doctor, company school, and even for sharpening tools, and the company sold alcohol to the miners at many pit-head wages offices.

It was against these conditions that James Keir Hardie fought. Born in Holytown, north of Motherwell, he went down the pits at the age of 10, at Newarthill in North Motherwell. Down the pit, he studied in his work breaks and learned shorthand by the light of his miner's lamp. Inspired by his reading, and noting 'I owe more to Robert Burns than to any man living or dead', Hardie agitated for miners' rights and was blacklisted in 1878, never working in the pits again. He took to trades union work, organising the embryonic Scottish Miners' Federation, of which he became secretary in 1886. He founded the Scottish Labour Party in 1888 and in the same year stood, and lost, in Mid Lanarkshire (which included Motherwell's neighbouring town of Wishaw), gaining only 600 votes. By this time Hardie had dropped his evangelical stance, though he retained a Christian outlook during his life. His conversion to socialism came on a visit to London in 1887, when he met Tom Mann, who introduced him to Friedrich Engels, Marx's co-worker. But Hardie never became a Marxist, remaining an ethical socialist all his life.

Thereafter, Hardie's work took him south and he was elected as MP for West Ham in 1892 and became the founder and leader of the Independent Labour Party (ILP) in 1893. Later elected for Merthyr Tydfil, a Welsh mining seat, he was instrumental in the establishment of the Labour Party in 1906. He was active in support of the miners and railway workers who were shot down and killed by the Liberal government in the industrial unrest of 1910–14. Hardie took an active part in the fight of international socialism against the policies of imperialism, and called for a general strike in response to the outbreak of any capitalist war.

When war loomed in 1914, Hardie organised demonstrations for peace. Then the First World War broke out, and the international socialist parties rallied to national defence. Hardie was devastated. Miners in his own constituency broke up his anti-war meetings and he died, of sorrow as much as anything else, in 1915 at the early age of 59. In the *Workers' Dreadnought* of that year, Sylvia Pankhurst (who had probably been Hardie's lover) described him as 'the greatest human being of our time'. It is difficult to think of a serious rival.

Thousands of miners in Wales, and in Lanarkshire, volunteered for the Killing Fields of Flanders and countless thousands never returned. In 1918, in both coalfields, May Day saw strikes against the continuation of war and for peace. Too late, the men Hardie had lived and died for saw the wisdom of his message against capitalist war. Humanity as a whole is still paying the price for the failure of the international socialist movement to oppose the imperialist slaughter of 1914. From that fatal decision, all the horrors of the 20th century subsequently flowed.

By 1914 conditions for the Lanarkshire miners had improved. A four-month strike in 1874, followed by a three-month strike against a 25 per cent wage cut in 1894 had both failed, the latter after running battles with police in north Motherwell and a public appeal for calm by the Provost, John Colville. But in 1899, the Lanarkshire Miners' Federation, led by Robert Smillie, won the eight-hour day after a strike when they were supported by the co-operative movement, which extended credit to the strikers. This was followed by the UK-wide 1912 strike – so solid in Lanarkshire that there was no picketing – when the miners gained a minimum wage, preventing the practice of savage wage-cutting in times of recession.

In the iron and steel trades, strikes in the 1870s had been defeated, but in 1886 the British Steel Smelters' Association – the first union in the industry – won a strike for union recognition against the iron and steel masters. Colville went personally to Wales to recruit blacklegs but when the train carrying them was nearing Motherwell, it was stoned and retreated. William Hodge, the union leader, persuaded the scabs (strike breakers) to return home, and the union paid their fare. Despite this victory, the iron- and steel-workers did not win the eight-hour day until 1918.

Motherwell Station would bear further witness to some of the most dramatic events in the Clydeside labour movement before the First World War. Fatalities were actually higher in the railways at this time than in steel working or coal mining, partly because of the long shifts that many worked (up to 15 hours a day). The Amalgamated Society of Railway Servants called a national strike in December 1890, and the Caledonian Railway Company responded by ordering the eviction of strikers and their families from their homes. When this was resisted successfully by a mass mobilisation across the entire Motherwell working class, troops were called in from Glasgow. An estimated 20,000 people

POLICE BATON CHARGE STRIKING RAILWAYMEN (1891)
Armed troops are in the background

39

turned out in response, occupying central Motherwell. They were baton-charged by the police, and in the ensuing fight, Motherwell Station was attacked and partially destroyed, making national headlines. The strikes were eventually defeated, but never again did Motherwell employers dare to use the eviction weapon, frequent hitherto, in a strike.

Despite this intense class conflict, the political labour movement was slow to develop in Motherwell. The parliamentary situation in North-East Lanarkshire, to which Motherwell belonged, was dominated by the forces of Liberalism before 1914. Apart from a 1901 by-election won by the Unionists, the Liberals held the seat from 1885 to 1914, often being represented by local employers, such as James Colville of the steel firm in the 1890s. Workers who had the vote generally supported the Liberals (Hodge of the Steel Union supported Colville, for example), though a minority of workers, especially in the skilled iron and steel trades, supported the Conservatives, through a Unionist Orangism. Sectarianism bedevilled Motherwell, especially in the period 1909–10, when there were widespread riots. Why was this the case?

Motherwell did not have a massive Catholic population. By 1900, Glasgow's Catholic minority was approaching 30 per cent. In 1881, 1,000 of Motherwell's 13,000 population were Irish, and even in 1911 it was only 4,000 out of 40,000 (about 10 per cent). Yet demagogues like Samuel Boal and Hugh Ferguson were able to stir up trouble and gain support in Motherwell that their sectarian kindred could not in Glasgow.

Possibly the answer lies in the composition of the local population. In Glasgow many of the immigrants came from far and wide, in Motherwell they overwhelmingly came from Lanarkshire, with its strong Covenanting Protestant traditions.

The 1881 census, according to Rob Duncan, shows that 'the local population which had been born and raised in Dalziel and the surrounding parishes... were the main elements of the local working class'. Aside from 1,000 each of Irish, English and people from the rest of Scotland, the town's population was from Lanarkshire. Motherwell was not a melting pot like Glasgow, but a town whose majority carried with them aspects of the religious thinking of their rural and village forebears. Indeed, when the ILP's newspaper, *Forward*, characterised Motherwell as a 'bibliopolis' in 1909, they were not alone. The *Glasgow Herald*, in 1913, spoke of Motherwell with its 'freak religions with their multitude

WORKERS COUNTER-ATTACK MOTHERWELL STATION
Its destruction made national headlines

of evangelists' as 'an indication of social ill-health' in the town. One of the 'freaky evangelists' was John Colville himself, head of the steel firm, provost, and later MP. A United Presbyterian, Colville conducted open-air street corner meetings for many years, formed a branch of the Glasgow Foundry Boys Church in the town and supported the setting up of the Young Men's Christian Association (YMCA). And things got freakier when John Maclean came to town. By 1919 Maclean had made himself famous, or notorious, for his opposition to the First World War, which had earned him several periods of imprisonment. He was also the most influential socialist propagandist of that time.

Socialists fight sectarianism in the working class with all the weapons at their disposal. A knife is a weapon, but it is essential to hold it by the handle, not the blade. When tackling sectarianism you start from what unites workers, not what divides them. Whether Maclean was mentally unbalanced by the time he came to Motherwell in 1919 matters not. Personally, I think his writings show the signs of paranoia, and also of an anti-working class Celticism verging on racism at this period. Consider this dreadful outburst:

> My desire is to prevent Scotsmen being used to smash our sister race, the Celts of Ireland, for English capitalists who are descended from the Germans. The Welsh, the Scots and the Irish are all of Celtic origin, so that from a racial point of view the Welsh and the Scots ought to line up with the Irish.
>
> *Vanguard*, July 1920

But judged purely politically, his intervention in Motherwell was disastrous. Instead of coming to the town to spread the message of the Russian Revolution, or to engage in some aspect of working-class industrial struggle, Maclean and his lieutenants came with a gospel of support for Sinn Fein. Before the war, Maclean had been very clear that 'Irish Labour would not be free under a Sinn Fein Republic' but by this time he had embraced Sinn Fein uncritically. But let the man speak in his own defence, reporting on the meeting in *Vanguard*:

When I told the crowd that the Sinn Feiners and Nationalist by vote in January had captured 'Derry, and that therefore 'Derry's walls had surrendered, this statement was too much for the hooligans who had come to enrage me.

The speakers were attacked, the platform collapsed and a riot broke out before order was restored.

But events were to turn more dramatic still. The post-war boom ended suddenly in Motherwell. At the height of the 1930s depression, over 50 per cent of men in Motherwell and Wishaw were claiming unemployment benefit, a total of 11,000 workers. But in 1922 the total of unemployed people in the two burghs, now united as a parliamentary constituency, was even greater at 12,000. This produced an extreme political volatility, as large numbers of workers were radicalised leftwards, whilst others were so in a different direction. In 1922 the labour movement candidate for Motherwell was chosen from the newly formed Communist Party, and Walter Newbold was supported by the local ILP in a United Front policy. Newbold triumphed with 8,000 votes (33 per cent) over a divided opposition of two Liberal candidates (one of whom was David Colville, the last steelmaster to contest the seat) and an Independent Conservative, Hugh Ferguson, who stood as an Orange Protestant.

It was decided that this 'blot on Motherwell' had to be wiped out, and a quite unprincipled coalition of right-wing forces did so in the election of 1924 when Newbold was defeated, despite raising his vote by 1,000 (four per cent). Colville withdrew, leaving his votes to the Conservative, the Orangeman Ferguson, now adopted by the official Conservative Party, and who narrowly scraped home. The Labour movement then decided to ditch Newbold and adopted a Protestant clergyman, the Reverend J. Barr of the United Free Church, to take the wind out of Orange sails, and he was elected in 1924. The seat remained Labour afterwards (despite a shock SNP victory in a by-election in 1945 during wartime) and Orangeism became, to quote Duncan, 'a cultural and a social, rather than a distinctively political phenomenon'. But just as the likes of Ferguson disappeared from the political scene, so too did people like Newbold. The next time the Communists contested Motherwell in 1929, they won barely 1,000 votes, and Motherwell, like the rest of Lanarkshire, sank into the miasma of 75 years of right-wing Labourism.

After 1945, the remaining mines in Motherwell were closed, but the steel industry went from strength to strength. Despite the downturn in shipbuilding in the 1960s, steel was able to take advantage of the post-war expansion in white consumer goods (washing machines, fridges) which the newly affluent working classes were able to afford, and also of the expansion of the Scottish car industry at Linwood and Bathgate in the 1960s. Far from being in a state of steady decline, the halcyon days of the Scottish steel industry were from 1950 to 1975, and this was marked by the building of Ravenscraig at Motherwell from the mid-1950s. When in full production, the steel mill employed 6,000 men, as many as the entire iron and steel industry in the town before 1914. With production of 1.5 million tonnes of steel a year, Ravenscraig alone out-produced the entire Scottish Victorian steel industry. This, too, was no rust bucket plant, but one of the most advanced in the entire world. Wages were high and, for the first time in their history, the people of Motherwell enjoyed prosperity and steadily improving housing conditions.

In 1980 the nationalised British Steel Corporation (BSC) offered its workers a two per cent wage deal, at a time of almost 20 per cent inflation, reverting to the classic 19th century tactic of wage-cutting. The first national steel strike since 1926 lasted three months, and with support from the railway workers and the miners, the steel workers settled for 12 per cent; still a wage cut, but less than envisaged. Then in 1984–5 came the miners' strike. The railwaymen blocked coal to Ravenscraig, and the plant was supplied with coal by scab lorries operated by Yuill and Dodds. The miners expected payback from the steelmen, but the latter were fearful for their jobs under the new Thatcher government, so they continued working with scab coal. Ravenscraig became the focal point of the miners' strike in Scotland, with daily and often violent clashes between miners' pickets and lorry drivers and steel workers. A massive police presence ensured that the coal got through.

Eventually, the miners were defeated. Thatcher congratulated the Ravenscraig men for working during the strike – and three years later privatised BSC. In the next four years, with jobs being cut again and again to 3,500, the men at the 'Craig broke all production records, reaching 2.5 million tonnes in 1990. Nevertheless, in 1992 the plant was closed, and steelmaking ended in Motherwell. Unemployment locally rose to 20 per cent and over the next decade the town's population fell back to about

30,000. In 1996 Ravenscraig was demolished. Following shortly afterwards, as a casualty of the butchery of the mines and the now obviously
short-sighted dash for gas in power generation, Anderson Strathclyde (as
Anderson Boyce had become) closed its coal-cutting machinery manufacturing plant, and Motherwell Bridge staggered close to liquidation.

Motherwell today

Motherwell Station does not look like a shrine to former proletarian
battles, nor does it look anything like the Victorian glass and iron palace
that was wrecked in 1890. Instead, 1970s angular ugliness rules, taken
from the same school of town planning that demolished much of
Motherwell town centre, put a ringroad around it and placed a shopping
centre on the resulting traffic island. On exiting from the station, to the
north lies Muir Street, at the end of which the splendid sci-fi cooling
towers of Motherwell Bridge's works can be discerned; they are worth a
digression to view closer. This works survived by drastic rationalisation
and by selling off the bulk of its closed factory site for housing, and is now
operating with a few hundred workers as MB Aerospace. All around Muir
Street in north Motherwell is council housing of high quality from the
inter- and post-war periods, with newer private housing.

But we are in Motherwell, and at Milton Street, the former centre of
Orangeism in the town, is the War Office Orange Lodge, and just past
this at Hope Street is the Masonic Lodge. Here, too, is the office of the
Motherwell Times, founded in 1883 and still surviving as a local paper.
A splendid church sits on the south side of Hope Street. This is formerly a
Free Kirk but now home to an evangelical Christian grouping. As we
said, we are in Motherwell. Heading south along Menteith Road, you
pass Merry Street, where some good examples survive of the poor quality
low-slung working-class housing that characterised much of the town
until the 1950s. Off Menteith Road, Park Street leads to the Dalzell
Works and its fine red-sandstone office block with its First World War
memorial and Colville emblems. This works is still operational, though
with fewer than 500 employees. It no longer makes iron or steel, but rolls
steel produced elsewhere, and is constantly threatened with complete
closure by its present owners, Corus.

Crosshill Street takes you over the railway and then Orbiston Street leads east through the former industrial area, now composed of trading estates, and brings you to the roundabout at Craigneuk Street. Here to the south lie some wonderful tower blocks, the colourful pagodas of south Motherwell, gracing the horizon. Indeed, the council housing in Motherwell is, on average, equal to the best that Glasgow erected. Craigneuk Street leads to the former Flemington Iron Works, now an industrial estate with half its tenancies unfilled. In front of it is the fine sandstone Craigneuk School, now being converted into flats. The Craigneuk area lies ahead, and was once the most overcrowded area in Motherwell and the focus of much of the radicalism of the early 1920s. Behind Craigneuk lies the site of the former Ravenscraig works, now being developed for a virtual new town of largely private housing. The deeply polluted site has had its arsenic, cyanide and other poisons buried under several feet of soil.

Back along Craigneuk Street leads to Windmillhill Street, just off of which, on the left, is Fir Park, the stadium of Motherwell Football Club. Normally a lower half of the Premier League team, the 'Well, still nick-named The Steelmen, has a solid following of about 5,000 supporters and has had its moments of glory. Curiously, these have coincided with the worst periods in Motherwell's history. The Steelmen were the only team outside the Old Firm to win the old Scottish 'A' Division from 1919 to 1939, and they did so in 1932, when half the town's population was unemployed. Their most recent success was winning the Scottish Cup in 1991 – the year it was announced that Ravenscraig would close.

Further on at the north side of Windmillhill Street lies the town's oldest building, the (now) South Dalziel Parish Church, rebuilt here in the 1790s. It is a very fine example of simple Scottish rural Presbyterian vernacular, and its graveyard is a green oasis in central Motherwell, with many interesting gravestones. The appalling effects of Motherwell's industrial pollution can be seen on many of these gravestones, which are not only faded and eroded, but in many cases the sandstone is actually holed straight through from the effects of the nearby steelworks, whose poisonous fumes undermined the memorials of the dead as it did the lives of the quick.

The staggering brutalism of Motherwell Civic Centre is complemented by that of the police station opposite, a little on from the church. These buildings are devoid of architectural pretensions to the point of genius. At the corner of Crossgill Street is a delightful wee MacFarlane cast iron fountain set in a tiny park. Its motto reads 'Keep the Pavement Dry', and it is the twin of the one which stands at Possil Cross in Glasgow, home of the MacFarlane foundry. A little further on, on the other side of the street in a kirkyard, is Motherwell's Hanging Cross, the truncated stump of one that reputedly stood where the former lairds of Dalzeil exercised feudal justice. The inscription engraved crudely on it reads 'Ye Olde x' and is probably a later addition.

The Colville-funded YMCA is on the right and Brandon Street ends at West Hamilton Street, where a simple sculpture of a pit head winding gear stands on the present ASDA supermarket site. South of here lay Watsonville, whose rich history the monument speaks of, but dumbly since the attendant signage had been broken off on my last visit. West Hamilton Street ends at Hamilton Road, where on the left stands the fine Carnegie Library, completed in 1906, with its motto 'Let there be Light'. Dunfermline-born Andrew Carnegie made his fortune in the United States and on his return to Scotland donated much money to provide libraries for the working classes. Opposite stands the solid Motherwell Town Hall, from 1886–7, now defunct, and sharing its main building between a pub and The Zone, Scotland's (apparently) biggest and best laser games site. Just beyond this lies the Motherwell Heritage Centre and Museum, sited in a reasonable new building, but surely the town hall should have been the place for such a provision? That said, the heritage centre is one of the best small museums I have visited, and a suitable place to end a tour of Motherwell's working-class traditions – as it lies just beside the station from which we started out.

Despite its harrowing by events of the last quarter-century, Motherwell is, as the town's publicity machine describes it, 'surprising'. The town, like Lanarkshire as a whole, has fared better than Glasgow in recent years, with its geographical position making it ideal for new commuter housing developments and its transport links also providing inducements to the retail and distribution parks that have replaced industry in contemporary Scotland. There are only pockets of the visible acres of dereliction and ubiquitous poverty ghettoes that are noticeable in Glasgow, or in Greenock for that matter. But there is little of the edge, of the excitement, of the gallousness, of Glasgow. Comparisons with Glasgow are perhaps invidious (though Lanarkshire's population is now as great as that of the Dear Green Place, at 600,000), but Motherwell produced no poets as Paisley did, no novelists as Greenock or Dumbarton did, and no great political figures bar Hardie, who spent over half of his life elsewhere. It did, however, produce legions of, now thankfully forgotten, cranky preachers.

CHAPTER 3

Coatbrig:
'The Strugglin', Toilin' Masses'

JANET HAMILTON NEVER wandered far from her native Langloan, later absorbed into the Iron Town of Coatbridge. Her longest foray was to walk into Glasgow in 1809 (when she was 13) to get married, and she returned the same day. She had taught herself to read at the age of five, but didn't teach herself to write until almost half a century later, when she began to publish her poems. She wrote of the area she inhabited in her poetry, but by the time she died in 1873, it had been completely transformed. In her poem 'Simmerlee', she observes:

> Oot-ower the auld brig, up up sweet Simmerlee.
> Sweet, said ye? – hech, whaur? – for nae sweetness I see:
> Big lums spewin reek an' red lowe on the air
> Steam snorin', and squeelin', and whiles muckle mair!
> Explodin', an' smashin', an' crashin', and then
> The wailin' o' women, an' groanin' o' men
> A' scowther't[1], an mangle't, sae painfu' to see –
> The sweetness is gane, noo it's black Simmerlee.

These wonderful lines give voice to the speechless victims of life in Coatbridge at that time, noting not only the hellish pollution, but also the appalling and dangerous conditions of the workers in the iron foundries. Indeed, in 1854, Robert Baird, one of the iron masters, was to admit of the Gartsherrie works in Coatbridge in 1854 that 'there is no place out of [i.e. except for] Hell worse than that neighbourhood'. However, as late as 1835, the newly established Monklands and Kirkintilloch railway was offering passengers from Glasgow 'rail pleasure trips to Airdrie, Gartsherrie and intermediate places'.

---

[1] *Scowther't*: burnt, scorched.

Although its close neighbour Airdrie had existed for some time, until well into the 19th century there was little, not even the name, where Coatbridge now lies. The Monkland Canal, the chief engineer of which was James Watt, had snaked out from Glasgow in the 1770s to carry coal from the small pits of North Lanarkshire to Glasgow, and lime to the agricultural improvers of the later 18th century countryside. One of these improvers was Alexander Baird, a local farmer, more a kulak than a peasant, who had several farms which he enclosed, and on which he established coal workings. Baird joined an agricultural club and held ploughing matches on his farm. Though he became moderately wealthy, it was not farming that established the Baird wealth – though it undoubtedly gave the family their commercial start and provided the capital for later developments.

The existence of the canal was almost providential when black-band ironstone was discovered in the Monklands area. Later, the hot-blast method of iron production would be patented by J. B. Neilson. The area now had everything needed for iron production, demand for which boomed with industrialisation. The district soon became the centre of Scottish iron production; the second largest in the UK. There were many producers in the Coatbridge area. The Neilsons themselves set up the Summerlee Ironworks, and the Carnbroe Ironworks was founded by James Merry. But the largest, with 16 blast furnaces, twice as large as any of the rivals, and by far the longest lasting, producing iron from 1830 until the mid-1960s, was the Gartsherrie iron works of William Baird and Company. Before this there had been only small local iron works, such as that at Faskine which built the first Scottish iron boat, the *Vulcan*, in 1818–19, which was used as a passenger vessel on the canal. But Gartsherrie was something different, producing 100,000 tonnes of pig iron a year.

Alexander Baird set up the company but almost immediately left it to the running of six of his seven sons. Although William gave the firm his name, the most important partner until his own death in 1873 was James Baird. The Bairds sought to avoid patent payments to Neilson, on the basis of improvements they had made to his hot-blast method of iron production. A lengthy court case ensued and the Bairds lost, paying Neilson a settlement sum of £106,000, equivelent to well over £1 million today. Baird – along with his brothers – had become so rich so fast that he was able to write a cheque for the damages on the spot. From Gartsherrie, the firm expanded to other iron works in Scotland and, with the coal and iron mines it owned, it employed 10,000 people by the 1860s. Of these, 3,200 were at Gartsherrie, where the waste bing was the size of the Great Pyramid in Egypt. It was in operation night and day, and one commentator noted:

> Anywhere in the streets of Coatbridge at night one could easily read a newspaper by the light of the furnace tops, where waste gasses were burnt off.

These gasses were rich in sulphur dioxide, which rainwater subsequently changed to sulphuric acid, a substance highly injurious to both buildings and people.

The wealth that the Bairds accumulated in 40 years begs belief. Each of the six brothers died a millionaire; James was the last to go, worth well over £1.2 million, in addition to the landed estates worth more than £1 million that were in family hands. These included Knoydart, which Baird bought in 1857. At the height of the iron boom in the early 1870s, the four then-surviving brothers shared dividends of over £1 million. The personal wealth of the extended Baird clan easily reached £1 billion in today's money. No Scottish industrialist, or industrial family, came near that in the 19th century, not even the Tennants of St Rollox.

As well as acquiring estates, the Bairds sent all their children to private English schools and universities to learn how to be country gentlemen, 'so that they might be able to live in a manner more becoming to their position and rank', as the will of the second Alexander Baird put it. Few of the Bairds were to play any further part in running the company, which was increasingly left to managers from the 1870s. One of the Baird legatees was Abingdon Baird, who managed to get through £3 million in seven years on horses (he owned 86 of them) and whores (Lily Langtree was his lover), before dying bankrupt in 1890. He had certainly learned how to behave in a manner befitting his rank, that of a parasitic rentier. The Bairds were staunch Conservatives, both William and James being members of parliament for the Falkirk burghs in the 1840s and 1850s. This seat included Airdrie, but not Coatbridge, which was not yet a burgh. The Bairds heavily funded the Conservative Party, helping to revive its fortunes in mid-Victorian Scotland, and were thanked by Prime Minister Benjamin Disraeli for their efforts.

COATBRIDGE TINPLATE WORKS, c.1900
The Iron Masters ensured that Coatbridge was exempt
from pollution control legislation

James Baird also left £500,000, known as the Baird Trust, to the
Church of Scotland for 'the mitigation of spiritual destitution among the
population of Scotland'. This money was not to be used for social or
welfare projects, but solely for the building of new churches in industrial
areas. It has been called 'the greatest fire insurance policy in history'.
Although they were doubtless too sanctimonious and self-satisfied for it
to ever cross their minds, if they existed, the fires of Hell would be prepared for the likes of James Baird and his brothers. For even amongst
the rapacious, brutal and hypocritical capitalist exploiters of Victorian
times, there are few to match the Bairds in the catalogue of misery they
inflicted upon thousands of people for so many generations.

A visitor to Coatbridge, named Bremner, described the area in 1869:

Dense clouds of smoke roll over it incessantly and impart to all
the buildings a particularly dingy aspect, and in a few hours the

visitor finds his complexion considerably deteriorated by the flakes of soot which fill the air and settle on his face. A coat of black dust overlies everything.

By this time various pieces of legislation had been passed which allowed burghs to take action against the pollution of the air and water courses caused by industry. The Bairds and other local iron masters fought successfully until 1885 against the granting of burgh status to Coatbridge, simply in order to be able to continue pollution at will. Even after 1885, the bill giving Coatbridge burgh status was only accepted by Baird and the others since a clause exempted 'furnaces, malleable works, collieries and tubeworks' from the Public Health Acts. Late burgh status also meant Coatbridge was delayed in receiving a public water supply, and well into the Victorian era many families used the polluted Monkland Canal, a carrier of cholera, for their drinking supply. The Bairds, and other iron masters, also saw to it that the working and living conditions of their workers were dreadful, even by the low standards of the times.

The iron masters erected housing for the influx of their workers, and this was of the most basic type – poor-quality houses in long monotonous rows, such as the Long Row at Dundyvann Works which was 600 yards long. The rows were built as near to the works as possible, on company land to avoid expense of land purchase. As Drummond and Smith describe them:

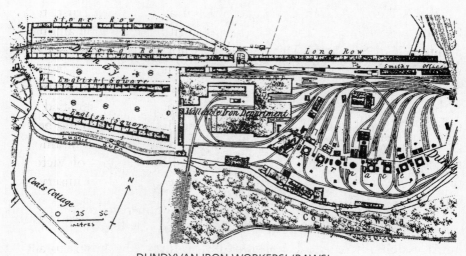

DUNDYVAN IRON WORKERS' 'RAWS'
Overcrowded, filthy, insanitary – and just next to the poisonous works themselves

The Carnbroe Rows, of Merry and Cunningham (built 1838) consisted of three single storey rows. The most westerly, known locally as the Monkey Row, consisted of 20 back to back single ends containing two hole-in-the-wall beds. The other two rows were room and kitchens. The rows were served by dry toilets, one common water pipe and open sewers (sheughs) until 1923... it was into the 1930s before gas was led into the rows, replacing paraffin lamps for lighting; electricity never got there before the bulldozer... the workers' rows were visited by recurrent eruptions of cholera and enteric fever (both contracted from polluted water), typhus fever (from lice) or endemic typhus (from the bites of rat fleas).

The Royal Commission on Housing reported in 1912 that the Rosehall Rows were 'single storey hovels', whose inhabitants kept coal under the beds (they had no baths!). The sanitary conditions, it was reported, 'were in a state of revolting filth'.

Bairds' rows lasted longest. Some were joined together into four-room homes with an inside toilet, and in the 1940s electricity was installed (at the tenant's own expense). The last of the rows at Gartsherrie were emptied and demolished shortly before the closure of the works in 1967.

Provision of housing was a useful tool of the employers for exercising social control, as eviction was a powerful weapon. This was used most often to break strikes, and the dominance of tied houses in the Lanarkshire iron industry meant that it was almost impossible to develop trades unions, fight for decent wages and improve conditions of labour. The Bairds were savagely anti-union and managed to keep Gartsherrie itself union-free, though not their iron and coal mines. Like most iron masters, they secured their own raw material supplies by owning local mines, and here the workers were more able to organise. All iron masters were anti-union. Hodge, the first leader of Scotland's iron and steel union, described the Nielsons of Summerlee as 'the most vindictive anti-union employers in the iron and steel industry'. Given the Bairds' record, the Neilsons must have been bad. A strike for union recognition actually occurred at Merry's Carnbroe iron works, but this was broken by the introduction of Irish and Highland strike breakers. Merry certainly didn't make his workers happy, they were forced to buy supplies at the company store (which sold at 10 per cent above local shop prices) or otherwise face eviction. Whatever their political (Merry was a Liberal and stood successfully against James Baird in 1857 in the Falkirk burghs) and economic disagreements, the local iron masters were able to establish a united front to keep wages low and prevent their workers organising.

In the wake of the establishment of the iron-producing works, which had a total of 60 furnaces in operation by the 1860s, came the malleable iron works, which turned the iron into a thousand different products. Some malleable iron works were actually attached to the iron producers in an integrated operation. However, this work was also mainly unskilled heavy labour, of which there was a limitless supply in the surrounding region, and conditions there were only slightly less bad, as these works were marginally less polluting than the actual foundries. Indeed, it took a long time before skilled manufacturing of any size took place in the Iron Burgh. Towards the end of the century, Lamberton's opened a works producing heavy industrial machinery for the iron and other industries. Murray and Paterson began manufacturing hauling equipment for the mining industry, and Stewarts (later Stewarts and Lloyds) opened a factory producing iron and, later, steel pipes. But the various high-polluting, low-paid iron works remained the main employers around 1900. By that time, the appearance of Coatbridge had not improved from earlier in the century. In 1894 it was described as 'a desolate, black district where nature's surface is scarified and loaded with rubbish heaps'.

In the 19th century, there could indeed have been few places outside Hell worse than Coatbridge. Blackguards like Baird assured that all would be well, would the workers only go to church and avoid drink. Others agreed, such as Archibald Allison Sheriff of the County of Lanark, who spoke of the workers in Monklands generally as follows:

Not one in 10, probably not one in 20 even thought of going to church on Sunday, but spent the day drinking in spirit shops, amusing themselves with dog matches or cock fights, or lounging about the fields or coppice woods with idle young women of their acquaintance.

Mr Baird of Gartsherrie has assured [me] that the local mining community spent upwards of £200,000 a year on hard liquor, while 70 per cent of his own workmens' wages were spent on drink, encouraged all the more by high wages.

What appalling cant! Company shops all stocked alcohol, and often at mines and iron works the spirit shop was situated next to the wage office, and drink sales brought in an additional profit to the masters and their agents. We can more admire Janet Hamilton in her poem 'Our Local Scenery', who also denounced the evils of excessive drinking, but she sees where 'the strugglin', toilin' masses' get their drouth from – the misery of their working lives:

> Smoorin' wi' reek an' blacken'd wi' soot
> Lowin' like Etna an' Hecla to boot
> Ought o' our malleables want ye to learn?
> There's chappin' an' clippin' an' sawin' o' airn
> Burnin' and sotterin'[2], reengin' an' knockin'
> Scores o' puir mortals roastin' and chokin'
> Gizen'd an' dry ilka thrapple and mouth
> Like cracks in the yird in a het simmer drouth
> They're prayin' puir chiels, for what do you think?
> It's no daily bread, it's drink, 'Gi'e us a drink!'

However, Sherriff Allison would soon get to know the miners of Monklands a little better.

The miners of Lanarkshire had a long tradition of struggle. Like others in Scotland, they had taken legal action to have their status as tied serfs abolished in 1799, and many took part in the reforming movements of that period, including participating in the Radical War and General Strike of 1820. Until about 1830, mining was a skilled father-to-son job in fairly small pits, and this was a daisy portion for the miners, when they could even control the length of their own working day. With the massive expansion of coal mining and influx of new labour to the coalfields, a downward pressure began on the miners' living and working conditions. Comparing the *Old* and *New Statistical Accounts* of Old Monklands parish from the 1790s to the 1840s shows that the number of coal miners increased from 400 to 4,000 in that period. Specifically

---

[2] *Sotter*: scorch or burn.

under attack were the miners' trades unions, which operated a virtual closed shop before the defeat of a long strike in 1837 which resulted in the breaking of their union. In that strike a policeman guarding scabs was killed and thrown down a mine shaft. But in the conditions of the 1840s, with the arrival of the Chartist movement, the miners decided to try and claw back their losses. One writer says that Chartism was 'an important though not determining influence on the miners' struggle', which was motivated by the desire to re-establish their unions and conditions of work and pay, destroyed five years before.

On 1 August 1842, 10,000 Lanarkshire miners came out on strike: 150 of the 200 pits which struck were in Airdrie (100 pits) and Coatbridge (50 pits), so Monklands was clearly the epicentre of the strike movement. This strike took place at a time when about 500,000 workers were on strike in Britain, the biggest strike before 1926. The movement was partly influenced by Chartism and the desire to gain the vote for working men, and partly by economic grievances. Despite the breaking of the union in 1837, the strike was solid and took the employers entirely by surprise, having been well prepared and secretly organised. The tactic was to hit the iron works (where the masters made most of their profits) as hard and quickly as possible. To do this the miners broke the law by not giving two weeks' notice of their action under the Master and Servant Act. This act, naturally, was always applied against workers and never against the 'masters' when they locked out, dismissed or evicted their workers. In engaging in a lightning strike, the men hoped to prevent the iron masters stockpiling iron and coal beforehand.

As well as being illegal in itself, the strike took a wide range of illegal actions. Menfolk would raid local farms by night and carry back food to their families; whole fields of potatoes were dug up while watchmen were held impotent. Women and children went round appealing for help for the strikes, and in the words of the *Glasgow Herald*:

> not content that the male portion of the turn-outs [i.e. strikers] should procure the means of continuing the strike by robbing the fields, the females have joined in bands, having their squalid children in their train, and forced everyone who was able, to give food or money.

In addition, some local shopkeepers gave the miners credit, hoping to wean them from the company stores after a victorious strike. Some workers left the area during the strike to work at the harvest; lifting tatties legally.

But against these tactics the employers had a more powerful tactic: the might of the state. Sheriff Allison had appeared in Airdrie as early as 4 August 1842 with 60 Glasgow policemen, and troops had been despatched there the previous evening. No-one in the town would give these unwelcome invaders accommodation, and Allison found all attempts to penetrate the strikers' organisation and identify ringleaders as useless. Despite his contempt for the working class, he had to admit that the miners were 'thoroughly and admirably organised'. His tactic was to try and arrest or intimidate groups of strikers or looters, and through severe example persuade the rest to return to work. On 8 August he issued a proclamation announcing that the illegal acts being committed 'amounted to Stouthrief[3] and are punishable by death or transportation' However, his efforts were, at first, unavailing.

The miners and their families had an excellent intelligence system, thousands of eyes were everywhere and Allison and the troops played a losing game against the strikers. In his own words, 'If we went out with the military one night, in one direction, we met no-one on the roads. Everything was perfectly quiet' – yet the same night in other areas bands of miners would have carried out successful plundering forays. A night raid was carried out on 265 miners' houses in Coatbridge for the purposes of arrest and Allison lamented that 'not one man was found in any of them'. The sum of Allison's efforts was the arrest of about a dozen men who were all given 60 days for stealing potatoes without the use of violence. By the end of August, many of the iron works were closed down or working on short time. (The heroic iron masters had all fled to the safety of Glasgow during the strike.) Individual coal masters broke ranks and conceded the four shillings a day that the miners demanded, as well as the reinstatement of fortnightly pay, instead of monthly. The miners who won the concessions went back, while the others stayed out and the unity of the strike was broken.

In a footnote to the strike, five miners were in Airdrie blockhouse on 20 September awaiting trial, and they were rescued by a huge crowd of

---

3   *Stouthrief*: theft with violence under Scots Law.

their fellow workers and released. Allison left Glasgow during the night and had the six ringleaders arrested, and escorted to Glasgow by troops who had arrived overnight from the barracks. The six men were transported into penal servitude, a savage and vengeful action on Allison's part, motivated by hatred and spite at his failure to break the struggle itself. Just a year later, the mine owners withdrew any concessions they had made in 1842, going as far as to evict 400 men, women and children from their homes at Dundyvann in midwinter, until they would return to work on the employers' terms, of 3s a day. The defeat of the miners and the 'iron grip' held over those in the furnaces by their employers meant that the Coatbridge area was never again to become a centre of class struggle in the 19th century. Indeed, its political and social history thereafter requires very little telling, in marked contrast to that of Motherwell in the previous chapter. What there is to relate, we will do en route round the former Iron Burgh.

Coatbridge today

Coatbridge Sunnyside is a station opened in 1888, and bears a strange name for one built in the shadow of 'dark Simmerlee' – and lying on the iron works' downwind side. The former site of this iron works lay derelict for 50 years and now contains the Summerlee Heritage Centre, a fascinating collection of items and displays from the past of Coatbridge and the wider industrial west of Scotland. A visit to this museum is essential for anyone visiting the town. (The entrance is on Heritage Way, on the west of the site.) Just north of the station is the Lamberton Works, still functioning and making automated engineering equipment. It is the last relic of the town's great industrial past. In the 1980s it made the then biggest industrial robot in the world for the steel industry, capable of lifting three-quarters of a tonne of red-hot iron. Further up Gartsherrie Road lies an industrial estate, which was built on the site of the Gartsherrie Ironworks, of which nothing any longer remains. Entering this industrial and trading estate is worthwhile only to show the huge size of the former Gartsherrie works.

Gartsherrie Road goes under a railway bridge and on the left is a council estate from around the 1970s, which stands on the site of the infamous Gartsherrie Rows. A left turn down Blair Road offers a couple of interesting possible diversions. First, on the left, is Lefroy Street, where, a century ago, there lived what there was of a middle class in Coatbridge. These fine mansions were occupied by managers of iron works, coal and timber merchants and solicitors. But it must have been lonely and rather frightening being a bourgeois in Coatbridge in the 19th century – there are a limited number of these dwellings and soon we are in artisans' housing and almost immediately into areas that were overcrowded slums a century ago.

Further down, on the right just after King Street, is a part of the Monkland Canal that is still not culverted, and a path along its north bank can be followed to a bridge that leads to the buildings of the Gartsherrie Home Farm. This lay on the lands of the Buchanans, Glasgow merchants who owned the Drumpellier estate. Blair Road leads to Bank Street, which brings us to the Langloan area, home of our poetess, Janet Hamilton. She is commemorated by a fountain in West End Park. Bank Street leads back towards the town centre, and on the right is probably the most monstrous building of the 20th century in a west-of-Scotland town-centre location: the Time Capsule Leisure Centre. You can avoid this by ducking down onto the walkway along the path of the old canal, which lies between Bank Street and West Canal Street. Hopefully, in doing so, you will not meet the same fate as that of an assembly of Orangemen who travelled the same route on 12 July 1857. They had arrived at Coatbridge Central Station, which lay at the far end of West Canal Street, and here follows a contemporary account of what happened.

> Unmistakeable evidence was apparent at Coatbridge during the day that the Catholics meditated an attack on the Orangemen on their arrival there. At an early hour in the evening many hundreds were congregated about the bridge leading to the railway station, where the Orangemen were to arrive by train. On their arrival, and having left the carriages, they proceeded down to the bridge, both bands playing, but having been informed of their danger if they walked through Coatbridge, they struck off on a path along the canal bank.
>
> They had not proceeded very far when they were overtaken by a dense mob who attacked them at the rear. The band members alone appeared to be the subject of the violent attack and several of

them were severely injured. The drums and instruments, to a considerable extent, were also destroyed.

Having dealt with sectarianism when looking at Motherwell, I was reluctant to take up the same issue again with Coatbridge, but it is unavoidable. Two factors made the religious conflict more severe here than in Motherwell, and more enduring. The first was that, unlike in Steelopolis, a strong labour movement capable of bridging the sectarian divide in a common struggle never really emerged in Coatbridge. The second was that, unlike Motherwell where Catholics were a very clear minority of the population, Coatbridge became the only town in Scotland where Catholics formed a majority of the population – currently at just over 50 per cent. Sectarian divisions in employment and also in housing continued here long after they were little more than memories elsewhere. But all signs show that over the last 30 years these divisions are being eroded, for example with mixed marriages in Coatbridge now rivalling the Scottish average of over 60 per cent rather than those of Northern Ireland (at 10 per cent).

After a roundabout, Bank Street gives way to Main Street, a pedestrianised area much in need of a makeover. The Main Street entry is flanked on the right by the Whitelaw Fountain, dedicated to an ancestor of the Willie of that name on whom Mrs Thatcher relied so much in the 1980s. The family hailed from here before heading to Cumbria to masquerade as country set. On the left is the local branch of the Airdrie Savings Bank, one of the many such credit institutions that developed for the artisan class of the 19th century, and almost the only one in the country to survive as an independent entity. It is a modest sandstone construction. Turning up Academy Street, there are more substantial buildings. This was an area feued by the Bairds and they set certain minimum standards for construction, so that today it still retains a pleasing feel, with its mix of modest villas and superior cottage-style dwellings. Here, also, is the Carnegie Library and, at Gartsherrie Place near the top of the hill, Gartsherrie Academy. This, a Baird endowment, is possibly the finest building in Coatbridge. Dropping down Church Street takes you back to Sunnyside Station. Waiting for the train, the words of Janet Hamilton might come to your mind:

It was sweet Simmerlee in the days o' langsyne
Whan through the wa'trees the white biggin' wad shine
An' its weel-tentit yardie was pleasant to see
An' its bonny green hedges and gowany lea.

Janet's world has gone, and so too has that which replaced it. The world of industrial Coatbridge deserves more than the neglect and sneering to which it has been attached, as do other industrial working-class towns that have suffered economically. The superficial 'worst places to live', 'architectural carbuncles' style of journalism so beloved of the Scottish press regularly places towns such as Coatbridge (and many others in this book) in these categories. Generations of working people made what was outwardly a hell into something habitable and even comfortable for themselves. They – and the current generation who mostly live worthwhile lives in conditions in which the sneerers could not survive for a day – deserve our respect.

CHAPTER 4

Life and Death
in Shettleston

IN 1885, THE ORDNANCE SURVEY *Gazetteer* of Scotland described
Shettleston as 'a somewhat poor and dingy place, inhabited chiefly by
colliers and agricultural workers'. Over a century later, the colliers and
agricultural workers have gone, but Shettleston retains some of the character described above. Though far in distance from Glasgow city centre,
the area shares some of the character of the run-down inner city – but
without the rich-built heritage of most of Glasgow's post-industrial districts. It is also (reputedly) the poorest place in the city, the poorest place
in Scotland, and the poorest place in the UK. Shettleston is apparently the
only place in Europe where male life expectancy is as low – at 66 years
– as it is in post-Soviet Russia. Retirement here is a gap year between life
and death.

Until 1912, when it was annexed by Glasgow, Shettleston was an
industrial Lanarkshire town with about 15,000 inhabitants, this itself a
tripling of population since 1891. Coal had always been mined here, but
the local lairds – the Craigs – expanded mining to meet the growing
demand in the 19th century, and re-built the now demolished Carntyne
House out of the profits. James Neilson was born in the village in 1792 and
he patented the hot-blast method of iron production, first established at
the nearby Clyde Ironworks, and this greatly increased the demand for
coal. Most of the pits were small; some, like the 'Dug Pit', where people
used to abandon unwanted dogs, appear to have been little more than
open quarries. Others had interesting names, like the Pricklismuir Pit,
known as 'Auld Prickie'. They were undercapitalised, liable to flooding
and were death traps to work in, being poorly ventilated and liable to
fire, damp and gas explosions.

In his *Memoirs of Shettleston*, written in 1930, Dan McAleer commented that:

All the pits in the district were badly ventilated at that time...
[*c.*1875] Miners in those days were old men at 40 and 50 years
of age... [In some collieries] the colliers received no money. There
was a store in Sandyhills where the miners got goods for their work.

The company store, operated under the truck system previously mentioned,
was a source of great profit to many mine owners. In some cases, they
took on unprofitable pits for the profits of the store. The miners of
Shettleston, like the others of the Lanarkshire coalfield, took part in
many struggles such as the Great Strike of 1894, through to the General
Strike of 1926. By 1930, however, the local thin seams were worked out
and flooding was such a problem that the last Shettleston mine, the
Greenfield Pit, had closed in 1929. The Lanarkshire coalfield – and the
area around Shettleston and its neighbouring pit village of Ballieston – was
to produce many of the leaders of the Labour movement in Scotland.

In 1900 Shettleston was not a pretty place, but those living and
working there did their best to make life tolerable. As well as the
Independent Labour Party (ILP), the co-operative had arrived in the
1890s, and there were socialist Sunday schools organised by the nascent
Labour movement. The town had an –apparently – excellent brass band,
and active Church choirs, as well as the Boys' Brigade. It had also seen the
establishment of the Shettleston Harriers in 1904, a phenomenally successful running club still very much in existence today and composed largely of
shopworkers in its early days. There was also the Shettleston Football Club,
established in 1903, which was less successful, never managing to win the
Junior Cup. The ability of working people a century ago to make tolerable,
social conditions that appear today as intolerable is quite remarkable.

Working people at this time were especially fond of walking, a cheap
and healthy recreation. With its semi-rural situation even between the
wars, Shettleston was a great place for a ramble. McAleer's *Memoirs* show
that, like many others, he regularly went for walks in the surrounding
countryside and he draws attention to a case that deserves to rank
beside those of Harvie's Dyke and Allan's Pend, as right-of-way battles
fought by working people in Glasgow. He mentions the attempts of the
iron companies to interfere with walking along the banks of the Clyde
from Carmyle to Kenmuir Woods, and tells us of the local opposition to
interference with the right to roam:

The agitators' battle was led by Davie Kirkwood with a determined gang of miners, labourers and tradesmen, etc... and [it]
kept the right of way path open to the public.

Frustratingly, no date is given for this conflict, though McAleer adds that
in 1930, Kirkwood, by then an ILP MP for Clydebank, won 'another
victory' when he raised in the Commons the issue of slag from a local
mine blocking the road, which led to its clearance.

By 1900, only 10 per cent of males were miners in Shettleston, and
a variety of factories came to the village to boost its population. The
railway reached the town in 1871, and this brought a flood of industry
to the village. J. and T. Boyd's Shettleston Ironworks opened in 1874, to
be followed by the Glasgow Ropeworks, and a large brickworks in the
1890s. A bottling works, chemical works, a steel foundry, a chemical works
and a sausage works soon followed. By the First World War, Shettleston was
a manufacturing town with a wide variety of medium-sized industrial
plants, employing largely semi-skilled or unskilled labour. In the conditions
of the time this meant low rates of trades union membership – and low
wages. Images in old collections of photographs show that working conditions in Shettleston's factories well into the 20th century retained a
Dickensian quality of horror. But if Shettleston workers were slow to
organise on the industrial front, they blazed the way politically.

A branch of the ILP was formed early in the village by the ex-miner
Thomas Simpson, who earned his bread after leaving the pits partly
through singing and playing at local village entertainments. Dan
MacAleer calls him 'the favourite dancer and singer in Shettleston'.
Simpson was also a leading light in the local brass band. The ILP found
a new recruit in 1907 in John Wheatley. Born in Ballieston, he moved to
Shettleston to work in the mines. Of Irish extraction, his early activities
were centred on the Home Rule fight, his energies later redirected to
socialist politics. Though remaining a practising Catholic all his life,
Wheatley was sanguine about the possibilities for the Irish masses under
an independent bourgeois Irish republic, and refocused his activities on
the Scottish working class. To attempt to draw the Catholic working
class into the growing Labour movement, Wheatley founded the
Catholic Socialist Society (CSS), which in some accounts is portrayed as
almost single-handedly converting the Irish immigrant community to

WHEATLEY'S HOUSING ACT 1924
This was the basis of social housing for the next half-century
and the one achievement of Labour in power between 1923 and 1924

socialism, whereas his biographer, Ian Wood, admits the CSS 'never claimed or achieved a mass membership'.

Indeed, though elected to Lanarkshire Council for Shettleston in 1910 (and serving in Glasgow's until 1922), Wheatley had trouble with the Catholic Church. In 1912 the local priest preached an anti-socialist sermon, and a catholic mob burned Wheatley in effigy and would have ransacked his house but for his courage in facing them down. By this time, Wheatley's house was a large villa outside the village, for he had abandoned the pits and after a career as a shopkeeper and (for a teetotaller!) spirits seller, he had set up a printing business and a newspaper, the *Glasgow Eastern Standard*. His business interests, and his later salary as an MP when elected for Shettleston in 1922, made him a moderately rich man. Aside from his villa and shares in the business, he left the modern-day equivalent of about £1.5 million.

Beatrice Webb met Wheatley several times and said there was something of the mobster (in a peaceful British context) about him. And indeed, Wheatley's money in printing came from his ILP and Labour Party contacts, as well as increasingly from the Catholic Church as they mellowed towards him. And even after he gave up his spirits licence, the teetotaller had economic links with the drink industry. He was severely embarassed when, in December 1926, the workers at his newspaper came out on strike alleging low wages – and this following a period when the *Glasgow Eastern Standard* had supported the General Strike and Wheatley had donated his MP's salary to the miners for the duration of the struggle. He was a man of contradictions, and supporters and opponents alike dubbed him 'Jesuitical' – not wholly uncritically, for all acknowledged his charismatic influence over others.

Wheatley opposed the First World War, on pacifist as much as internationalist lines, and took part in the campaign against conscription. But he then nefariously brokered the deal that emasculated the Clyde Workers' Committee (CWC) in 1916 during the dilution strike. He used his influence over David Kirkwood, shop stewards' convenor at Parkhead Forge, to push through dilution and break the united front of the CWC. He supported the 40 hours' strike that erupted in Glasgow and the west of Scotland after the First World War – but from the safety of the City Chambers, where he saw out the 1919 George Square Riot. Wheatley avoided the subsequent prosecution of some of the strike's leaders.

Wheatley's triumph in Shettleston in 1922 was part of the so-called Red Clydesiders' victory, which saw 10 left-wing MPs returned to Westminster from Glasgow. (Shettleston then included the district of Parkhead within its parliamentary boundaries.) Wheatley won almost 60 per cent of the vote and one of his opponents was Guy Aldred, who won only two per cent. Aldred was an interesting character, a charismatic Englishman who adopted Glasgow as his base for lecturing about anarchism in plus fours and tweeds. His ideology was an incoherent mix of anarchism and secularised Christianity, and he attracted, as such people do, a tiny band of acolytes, but no real following. Though an anarchist, he repeatedly stood for parliament on an anti-parliamentary platform, though that was the least of the contradictions in his political make-up.

Glasgow anarchism has a long and interesting pedigree, and has an almost continuous presence in the city since the arrival of Kropotkinite Jewish immigrants in the 1890s. Aldred himself was active until his death in the early 1960s, and I remember encountering the Glasgow anarchists later in that decade on visits to the city. In contrast to the then hippyness of anarchism elsewhere, these were mostly working men, and highly self-educated. They had a fringe element, though, of hard-looking guys in cheap suits and collar and ties, who said very little but apparently applied literally the anarchist dictum that 'Property is Theft' – and reversed through illegal activities some of the capitalists' expropriations. But we digress from Shettleston.

In parliament, Wheatley was given the health portfolio by Ramsay MacDonald in the first, minority, Labour government of 1924. His main achievement was the Housing Act of that year, which provided for the creation of mass public housing, subsidised from taxation, and was the basis of the slum clearance programmes of the 1920s and 1930s. But at the same time, he was able to stonewall in the face of Labour's commitment to sex education and contraception, despite enormous pressure brought to bear on him. He was disillusioned by Labour's failure in 1924 and did not join the second MacDonald government of 1929. With Maxton then a close political ally, Wheatley appears to have felt that the ILP should have cut its links with the Labour Party. Indeed, Beatrice Webb, who saw him as an ill man before his death, said of him: 'He would be a Communist if he were not a pious Catholic.' His funeral in 1930 was the biggest political funeral in Glasgow since that of John

Maclean, but there was no representative from the hierarchy of the Catholic Church present, despite his devotion to that organisation.

If Wheatley was drifting away from the Labour Party towards his death, one of his converts to socialism would, from a position to the left of Wheatley, drift far to the right, and be one of the architects of Labour's eventual domination of Glasgow politics. Patrick Dollan was in many ways similar to Wheatley. Born of Irish immigrants in Ballieston, and moving to Shettleston to work initially in the local rope works, and then in the mines, he later became a full-time journalist with the ILP newspaper *Forward*. Dollan joined the Shettleston ILP when Wheatley was its leader. As well as pacifism and teetotalism, Dollan, unlike Wheatley, embraced secularism and renounced his Catholic faith in 1911. He was more directly involved in the struggles of the First World War than Wheatley, and was imprisoned for his activities.

Elected to Glasgow Council for Govan, he became the leader of the Labour group, and was a great organiser who led the party to its becoming the biggest in the city in 1933, and to himself becoming Provost in 1938. But Dollan had become increasingly right wing, and when the ILP disaffiliated from Labour, he did not follow, instead organising the Scottish Labour Party to counteract the ILP's influence north of the border. He became a fervent recruiter for the armed forces as Provost, and after an illness, underwent a religious reconversion in 1941 – the year he accepted his knighthood – thus fulfilling the prophecy of John Maclean that 'he would be Sir Patrick before he was Saint Patrick'.

Wheatley was followed as Shettleston MP by John McGovern, who, surprisingly, had been Guy Aldred's election agent in Shettleston in 1922 and was later associated with Aldred and Harry MacShane in the 1930s in the Free Speech movement that led to the lifting of the ban on political meetings in Glasgow's parks. In the 1930s, McGovern supported the hunger marches and protested in parliament against the means test and cuts in welfare provision. When the ILP crumbled after the Second World War, he switched to the Labour Party and became increasingly right wing, ending as a fervent monarchist, opponent of 'godless communism', and supporter of moral rearmament, as indeed had Dollan. With Dollan and McGovern, 'Catholic socialism' had finally found its true resting place.

The ILP dominated Glasgow Labour politics between the wars of the

WORKING-CLASS MATERIAL CULTURE
A Co-op teapot. Until the 1960s, the Co-ops were the most important institution in the lives of working-class people

last century, to such an extent that – unlike in, say, Greenock or Motherwell – there was little space for the Communist Party to operate in the city as a left-wing force. But by the outbreak of war in 1939 – which it opposed – the ILP was a largely spent force. Cliff Hanley's amusing book, *Dancing in the Streets*, talks of the ILP in Shettleston and Tollcross during the Second World War, in a chapter entitled 'The Gutters will run with Tea', as follows:

> Even with wartime rationing, the ILP in Glasgow went through whole plantations of tea... We devoted our energies to eternal questions, such as who was prepared to be minutes secretary and what to do about arrears in the payment of dues.

In the 1930s, Hanley had moved from the Gallowgate tenements to Shettleston, to the area of Sandyhills, where some of the first – and best – of the cottage houses built under Wheatley's Act had been constructed. The area's semi-rural character, even in the 1920s, meant that there was much available land, and soon large housing estates linked Shettleston to previously separate districts such as Tollcross. The area's population continued to grow and reached its peak (as did Glasgow's at 1,050,000) in 1951 when Shettleston had, coincidentally, 51,000 people. Industrial decline led to population loss and today Shettleston and its satellites have about 30,000 inhabitants.

Present-day Shettleston

Much has gone from Shettleston, but the railway station, which opened in 1871, is still there, though now unmanned. Coming from Glasgow, it is worth pausing awhile on the overpass bridge and looking north (for we are heading south). To the north were collieries, such as the Greenfield pit, whence a tramway carried coal to the railway. To the west of the station, on its northern side, was found the Shettleston

Ironworks and further west of that, the Greenfield Brickworks. The Ordance Survey map of 1910 shows little housing on this side of the railway, apart from the tenements of Budhill Avenue and Budhill Square – and very fine these buildings are. They have been renovated and the square has been landscaped. When constructed around 1900, however, these buildings consisted not of two flats to a landing as now, but of three room and kitchens and one single-end, resulting in an enormous population density.

Leaving our bridge belvedere, an exit south takes you to Annick Street, formerly Station Road. Industry crowded round the railway, both north and south, on land today covered by trading estates, whose workers are moving goods made elsewhere, not locally. To the east of Annick Street stood the Glasgow Ropeworks, where Dollan briefly worked, and the Acme Steel Foundry, facing Gartocher Road. On the west was a saw mill and the North British Bottleworks. It is surprising that anything survived the redevelopment here, but on the corner of Old Shettleston Road is the Art Nouveau Eastbank Parish Church by Rowan, dating from 1904 and notable for its fine interior woodwork. A walk along Old Shettleston Road takes you to Wheatley Drive and Wheatley Road, warehousing on the site of the old bottle works, and then to the stadium of Shettleston Football Club, looking in a very run-down state. Until the 1960s, junior football had a large following, and teams like Shettleston could expect crowds of up to 5,000 people, the kind of attendances that the likes of Motherwell or St Mirren experience today.

Further along, you come upon a surprising relic of the past – a functioning factory, just before the end of Old Shettleston Road. This was initially Carntyne Dyewood Mills, and later became McGrouther Watt's sausage factory, and is now Freshlink Foods. At this point we come to Shettleston Sheddings, where the Old Shettleston Road joins Shettleston Road, formerly Main Street. The old Scots term *sheddings*, or *sheddens*, for a parting of the ways, is also found in nearby Parkhead. I tested the *patois* of a couple of local punters outside a pub called Sheddens and asked them where Shettleston began and Parkhead ended. 'At the gushet' was the reply: an old Scots word, yes, but not as old as the apparently now forgotten one that graced the pub they patronised.

Not even the most devoted Shettlestonian could claim that the place's main thoroughfare is a thing of beauty. With its extension into the former Eastmuir Street, it is a mile of, surprisingly, continuous (especially on the south side) turn of the 19th- and 20th century tenements of moderate quality. There is little to detain the eye in what is an overwhelming impression of grimness. This is relieved on the corner of South Vesalius Street, where a motif of clasped hands and the word 'UNITAS' on the wall denotes the former co-operative tenements. Its shops are no longer below the flats, but the Co-op retains a presence in Shettleston a little further along Shettleston Road. As was usual in areas like this, the best tenements lined the main thoroughfare. To the north and south of the former Main Street were the poorer ones, and here they were all demolished and replaced by dreadful cheap 1920s and '30s council housing. Today, most of this lies vacant and boarded.

Where the main thoroughfare joins again with the Old Shettleston Road, there is an interesting building. This is Eastbank Academy, opened in the 1890s as the main school in Shettleston. But this fairly modest structure apparently didn't appeal to the locals, who liked their architecture simple, and it was called 'Scott's Folly' after the then chairman of the school board. It was this school that Cliff Hanley attended in the 1930s. For a while it was occupied by the John Wheatley College – rather ironically, since he chose not to send his children to Eastbank but to give them a private Catholic education in a Jesuit school in Glasgow. Now, however, the former school is office units and the John Wheatley has moved to a new campus in Haghill, a couple of miles to the west, where Wheatley had no political presence. The new Private Finance Initiative-funded Eastbank Academy lies to the south of the old one. It does not look as if it will last as long as its predecessor.

Continuing along Shettleston Road one reaches the Kirkhouse Inn, claiming to date from 1771. On the same side of the road is an interesting graveyard, where the stone sentry boxes, built to watch against grave-robbing 'Burkers', are still visible. The gravestones date back to the 1750s. The old Shettleston Church stood here, a fine building dating from the 18th century, endowed by local benefactors such as the tobacco lords of the Bogle family, but the kirk has sadly been long demolished. The Glasgow Ropeworks site stood behind the graveyard wall.

South down Killin Street and then west along Ardgay Street takes you through the Shettleston of Wheatley's Housing Act. These are streets of excellent cottage houses, four in a block, with front and rear gardens.

Many have been sold to their occupiers, and hereabouts it is difficult to equate the image of Shettleston as the sick man of Europe with the visual reality. Ardgay Street ends at what might be considered Shettleston's finest building. Shettleston Hall, built just north of the Tollcross burn and thus within Shettleston, is a decent solid structure with architectural flair. It was built, with the adjacent public library, in the 1920s by the Glasgow Council's Office of Public Works and is influenced by no less than Christopher Wren's Hampton Court. Wellshot Road takes you back to Shettleston Road, and then Fernan Street leads to Carntyne Station and the end of our walk through Shettleston's past.

Shettleston, when compared with, for example, Cathcart, shows us the enormous variety of the proletarian experience, in Glasgow as elsewhere. The fact that the workers here aspired to, and in however a faulted manner achieved, a common political and industrial cause with those elsewhere whose living and working conditions were profoundly different lends support to Marx's conception of the class struggle as the motivational force of history.

CHAPTER 5

Easterhouse:
Altered Images

I HAD THOUGHT of including a chapter in this book on what became of the diaspora from Glasgow's inner city, older industrial areas even before the Easterhouse Question came to figure almost as prominently as the West Lothian Question in political affairs. Ever since Iain Duncan Smith visited the housing scheme in 2006, and was so appalled at what he saw that he tried to resuscitate One Nation Toryism, Easterhouse has featured in the political debate of this country. Unlike Mr Duncan Smith, I know Easterhouse quite well, and I also know that its fall into its darkest days in the 1980s came during the government of his predecessor, Mrs Thatcher, whose policies destroyed local employment and undermined social housing.

What images does the word Easterhouse conjure up when you hear it? Usually gangs, ice cream wars, drugs, poor housing, poverty, unemployment or 'a desert wi' windaes', as Billy Connolly described Drumchapel, Easterhouse's sister scheme on the other side of Glasgow. I say 'images' because it is almost certain that unless you live in Easterhouse, you will have never been there. The scheme is bypassed by all major road and rail links, and has little employment to draw in outsiders. And the only place where Easterhouse features in the media is the Bad News section.

I would never deny that these commonly held images are ones which resonate with the reality of Easterhouse, though often in an exaggerated manner. This is Easterhouse, not Rio de Janeiro or Johannesburg, for heaven's sake! But there are other realities here, and it is time that the message is put across that Easterhouse is 'more than just a scheme', as the subtitle of a project carried out by the Trondra local history group, expressed it.[1] What about history, culture, education and the arts for

---

[1] Hidden Histories; Greater Easterhouse, More than Just a Scheme. Trondra History Group, 2002. Aside from the personal encounters, all quotations from Easterhouse residents come from this work.

alternative images of Easterhouse? You have already heard the bad news – to hear something different, read on.

At its peak, Easterhouse was Western Europe's largest social housing project, and like many, a 'best laid scheme', which seemed a good idea at the time, it would later 'gang agley'. After the Second World War, there was a demand for social justice, in which housing figured prominently. Nowhere else was this more so than in Glasgow, which had some of the worst and most overcrowded housing in Europe: parts of the city had population densities close to that in Calcutta. The idea was to shift the population to healthier locations in the suburbs, where houses with baths, toilets and gardens would replace the old slums. As one of the new residents from the 1950s recalled: 'Two bedrooms, a living room and a separate kitchen. And a bathroom! It seemed like a palace to me.' Kids would have fresh air, and be able to play in the countryside rather than in rat-infested back courts.

The problem with Easterhouse, and with Glasgow's other satellite schemes, was that, although they were as big as the new towns like East Kilbride being built, they were not new towns. Instead of being overseen by centrally funded, government-underwritten new town development bodies, they were financed by a fairly impoverished Glasgow Corporation. Such a lack of financial clout meant houses could be built but there was little money or power to direct infrastructure to the schemes.

By the early 1960s, Greater Easterhouse had in excess of 40,000 people, more than present-day Perth or Inverness. There was one doctor and no dentist. There was one library, built in that year, but no swimming pool or cinema. There were no banks (even in 1990 one cash machine served 30,000 people). There was no police station. There were almost no shops, only (expensive) vans that came round the doors. There was little public transport, in an area where car ownership is still very low and was then almost non-existent. Most of all, there was not a great amount of local work, except for those lucky enough to gain employment at the small Queenslie Industrial Estate, where Weir's Pumps, with 900 workers, and Olivetti (who made typewriters in the 1960s), with 1,000 employees, were the largest employers. One ex-worker at Olivetti recalled: 'I really enjoyed it. There was a brilliant sense of cameraderie, and the pay was good.'

But most people in Easterhouse had to commute long distances (at a cost) to their former workplaces. Similarly, for many years there was inadequate schooling provision, and many children were bussed back to their old slum schools. Mothers took the bus (expensive and time consuming) back to Shettleston or Bridgeton in Glasgow's east end to do their shopping and fathers returned to pubs and clubs there. Many people thus found their disposable incomes reduced.

Worse still, it became apparent that the materials with which the houses had been built (concrete blocks and metal window frames) made them cold, damp and very expensive to heat. The housing stock began to deteriorate faster than the old tenements, and soon large parts of the scheme were impossible to let. As one resident recalls:

> Our new homes were upmarket compared to the slums we came from. We now had electricity, an indoor bath and our own bedrooms. But it didn't take long before these houses were as bad as the ones we came from due to dampness of the walls and condensation on the windows. They cost more to heat that the old slums.

When the economic recession of the 1980s began, most of the factories in the Queenslie Estate, including Olivetti and Weir's, closed their doors. The trickle of people from schemes like Easterhouse became a flood, and the population plummeted. By 1990, Easterhouse had such a bad reputation that the philanthropic entrepreneur Anita Rodick, known for her poverty initiatives, diverted her attention from the Third World and set up a Body Shop factory in Easterhouse, whose needs were deemed to be of Third World levels. It was in the 1980s and 1990s when drugs came to Easterhouse, fuelling the notorious Ice Cream Wars of the time. A dream died in Easterhouse. But today things are changing – new dreams, possibly more realisable, are being created, and the outside world should be told about them, and people encouraged to go and see for themselves.

When Glasgow acquired the area from Lanarkshire in the 1930s, Greater Easterhouse was a scattering of mining and small industrial villages around the Monkland Canal, which connected the iron deposits of Lanarkshire with Glasgow's industry. The canal was still open when Easterhouse was built and it provided an outdoor playground, through a dangerous one, for the local kids, who hung swings from the bridges and made rafts to navigate the canal course. One resident recalls, 'A pal of mine drowned in the canal, he had wellingtons on and he just slipped in and went under.' In the early 1970s, the canal was filled in and the M8 motorway built over its course. The area was also known for its many small landed estates with associated mansion houses, after which many of Easterhouse's sub-divisions are today named. Most of these villages and mansions disappeared with the unfolding of the Easterhouse plan.

One, however, remains. The historically unique Provan Hall still stands and is at the heart of the Easterhouse community, connected with many initiatives. And yet, financial restraints mean it is closed at weekends. If you are unable to visit during the week, a great way to see Provan Hall – and Easterhouse's other attractions – is to get the free bus from George Square that Glasgow City Council provides on Doors Open Day in September every year, which provides a drop-on/drop-off service to various buildings, including Provan Hall. This is the best place to start as it is the oldest house in Easterhouse; indeed, as the locals will proudly tell you, it is (depending on sources used) the oldest house in Glasgow and without doubt the finest pre-Reformation mansion house in Scotland. Yet I have still to find many of my Glaswegian associates, never mind outsiders, who know that Provan Hall even exists.

Provan Hall dates from about 1460. The prebendary of Provan was associated with Glasgow Cathedral, and King James IV hunted in the surrounding woods when he was a canon of the cathedral. Mary, Queen of Scots is reputed to have stayed at Provan Hall when visiting her sick husband in Glasgow, and there is a local well, reputed to be Mary's Well, where she supposedly watered her horse. The original hall has a dairy and kitchen downstairs, the latter with a fine vaulted roof and a fireplace capable of roasting a whole ox. Upstairs are the dining quarters and bedchamber. The curtain wall was added during the troubled times of the 17th century when the then owner Robert Hamilton, an ardent Royalist, needed help against the local staunchly Covenanting popula-tion. The house later passed to a tobacco lord, James Buchanan, who remodelled the hall according to his plantation in the West Indies, adding complex Blochairn House, which today forms the southern part of the hall. Buchanan's descendants, the Mather brothers, were born in the hall and died there as its last occupants in 1934.

But Provan Hall is not just about history, it is about the present. The house passed to the National Trust in the 1930s, but very little was sub-sequently improved. It is only in the last few years, with management

DESERTED,

FROM his Master's house in Glasgow, on the morning of Saturday the 3d current,

A NEGRO MAN.

He is about 35 years of age, and 5 feet 9 or 10 inches high, pretty broad and stout made, broad faced, and somewhat yellowish complexioned. The white of his eyes are remarkably tinged with black, and he has a surly gloomy aspect. His dress when he ran off, was an olive coloured thickset coat, jacket and breeches, a black wig tied behind, and silver buckles in his shoes; but as they were all good, it is probable he would change them for worse, and thereby supply himself with cash.

His name is THOM, but sometimes he assumes the name of THOMAS DIDDY.

A Reward of FIVE GUINEAS, and payment of all reasonable charges, is hereby offered to secure the said Negro in any jail in Scotland, so as he may be kept safe, and delivered to his Master's order. The money to be paid by Mr John Alton merchant in Glasgow, upon notice being sent to him of the Negro's being secured.

All shipmasters are hereby cautioned against carrying the said Negro abroad; and if any person harbours him, or assists him in making his escape, they will be prosecute therefor.

HAND BILL FOR ESCAPED SLAVE
In the 18th century the Buchanans, using money made from West Indies slave plantations, remodelled Provan Hall and added Blochairn House

taken over by Glasgow City Council, that the hall has begun to flourish again. Extensive and expensive repairs have been carried out to the building and the grounds landscaped and developed as a wildlife oasis. School pupils regularly visit the building, and in 2003 took part in a pageant to commemorate the 500th anniversary of the marriage of James IV to Mary Tudor in 2003. The Trondra Group, previously mentioned, is based in the hall, as is a volunteer gardening group, which works on the grounds and the vegetable garden.

When visiting Provan Hall, it always strikes me as sad that there are so few people there, especially when, just outside of the hall's grounds, thousands of people are shopping at the new Fort centre. Though no devotee of the new secular religion of shopping, I am a great admirer of the dramatic architecture of this titanium-clad Fort building. However, it would be good if some of the shoppers took the short stroll or drive to Provan Hall to see what else Easterhouse has to offer. Could the owners and occupiers of the Fort not give something back to Easterhouse by directing people to Provan Hall?

The other great secret asset of Easterhouse in Bishop's Loch, and a ramble to there from Provan Hall gives a good impression of the changes taking place in the area. Walking along Auchinlea Road, you can see both the old '50s housing, often derelict or in disrepair, and the renovated housing of today. Some housing is restored as social housing, and some has been sold as low-cost owner occupier units. In Auchinlea Road you also come across what they omitted to put into the scheme when it was built – a sports centre and a health centre. Westerhouse Road takes you past the Township Centre, a rather insipid 1970s style complex, and to the recently opened and much more striking John Wheatley College. This is an annex of the mother college in Glasgow's east end, and is named after John Wheatley, the Shettleston-born local MP in the 1920s, who as Minister for Housing in the first Labour government laid the basis for the provision of a social housing policy in his Housing Act of 1924. Due to the involvement of the John Wheatley College in training schemes up to 80 per cent of jobs in the 'Fort' have been taken by local people

It was not just original architectural thinking that went into this building, but also original social thinking. It was placed here as an annex of the main college in Shettleston to make it easier for local people to attend, but the college has doubled up as a one-stop shopping place with Easterhouse Library and swimming pool, which are located in the building. The theatre located in the college complex is used in courses for media students, and also duplicates this function for public arts performances by a local company, Platform Arts. In keeping with its aims, the whole complex is called The Bridge. I never thought I would see the day when I would go to Easterhouse to see and hear Stravinsky's *Soldier's Tale*, but it did happen. The National Theatre of Scotland Young Company is based here, which caused much mutterings in certain circles, but is a venture deserving of support. After all, Easterhouse has already produced *Lord of the Rings* star Billy Boyd from its ranks.

A trip to The Bridge at night in winter is a strong recommendation. Then, you can see the megaliths of Greater Easterhouse, Cranhill and Garthamlock Water Towers, illuminated as though some spaceships from Mars had just landed. Cranhill Water Tower is also the location of a sensory garden, created by local schoolchildren. These illuminations have added a great deal of cheer to the surrounding areas, especially on dark winter nights.

Down Lochend Road and Auchengill Road, one sees the same combination of regeneration and degeneration in the housing stock, until you suddenly leave Easterhouse and Glasgow behind, at the stunning Bishop's Loch. Easterhouse is surrounded by lovely countryside, of little use until now except as dumping grounds and drinking dens. That, too, is changing. The city council, in collaboration with the Forestry Commission, has spent a lot of time, effort and money in developing, waymarking and maintaining a set of trails in the Greater Easterhouse area and their leaflet, *The Woodlands of Easterhouse*, is astonishing in revealing the amount of woodland and loch scenery there is in and around the scheme. Local rangers lead regular walks, and work with local schoolchildren in getting them active and out into the countryside.

From Bishop's Loch there is a waymarked trail through Craigend Wood that will take you back to Easterhouse township centre; otherwise, you can follow the western edge of the loch to the former Gartloch Hospital, whose towers loom tantalisingly across the loch from Easterhouse. This was opened in 1890 as one of the main mental hospitals for Glasgow, and continued as such until the mid 1990s, when closure led to gradual decay in the building. Today, the hospital is being restored as luxury flats. These may be beyond the income of the residents of Easterhouse, but at least they will be within Glasgow's boundaries and contribute to the city's tax base.

There is a long way to go in Easterhouse. But part of its successful steps towards regeneration can be gauged by the simple fact that the area is not one of those notorious seven out of the poorest ten in the UK lying within Glasgow's boundaries. Finally, after half a century, Easterhouse is possibly a more pleasant place to live than many of the areas from which its inhabitants originally came.

CHAPTER 6

The Garngad:
Heaven and Hell

AT THE SUMMIT of Garngad Hill, the splendid spire of Townhead and Blochairn Church reaches for heaven. Although the church, built in the 1860s and formerly containing interior decorations by Cottier and Morris, is gone, the spire, which, at 250 feet, was once the highest point inside Glasgow's city boundaries, remains. But even when the church was built, another structure in the area reached nearer to heaven than the summit of its spire. Though it was built at the foot of the Garngad Hill at not much above sea level, Tennant's Stalk, or Tennant's Lum, was at one time, at 435 feet, the fourth highest construction on Earth. The chimney predated the church, being built in the 1840s, and was designed by Professor Rankine of the University of Glasgow to carry away the noxious fumes from the St Rollox Chemical Works, at the time the largest chemical works in the world. Though it might have come closer to heaven than the kirk spire, the lum and the factory it served brought its workers and those who lived around it much closer to an earthly hell.

The interior of the St Rollox works was described in 1847 by George Dodd, in *The Land We Live In*, shortly after 'THE Chimney' – as he designates it – was built:

> They are, necessarily, black and dirty, and as infernal in appearance as we can well imagine any earthly place to be. The heaps of sulphur, lime, coal and refuse; the intense heat of the scores of furnaces in which the processes are going on; the smoke and thick vapours which dim the air of most of the buildings; the swarthy and heated appearance of the men; the acrid fumes of sulphur and the various acids which worry the eyes, and tickle the nose and choke the throat; the danger which every bit of broad-cloth incurs of being bleached... form a series of notabilia not soon to be forgotten.

ST ROLLOX CHEMICAL WORKS IN THE MID-19TH CENTURY
A dark, Satanic mill if ever there was one

Luckily for those condemned to labour at St Rollox, it was only 400 yards from Glasgow's Royal Infirmary, where legions of workers went to receive medical attention throughout the lifetime of the works, which operated until the mid-1960s.

The deleterious effects on its workforce's health were accompanied by a similar effect on the local population. Despite the Stalk, the works continued to rain down pollution of all sorts on the surrounding area. The water courses of the local Forth and Clyde Canal, as well as of the nearby burns, were used as locations for despatching the effluent of chemical processes, while the solid residue was simply dumped on a site landward of the works. Earth, water and air were all laden with the by-products of the production of bleaching powder, caustic soda and sulphuric acid.

Nowadays, the image of the chemical industry evokes the idea of a science-based, advanced technological procedure; in the 19th century it was not so, and chemicals represented the lower depths of capitalist exploitation, involving almost entirely unskilled heavy manual labour in its production processes. The tennants also preferred what we would now regard as child labour. In the 1860s 50 per cent of the workforce of 1,600 were aged between 12 and 16, ie. they were boys. As well as causing the widespread pollution noted, chemical employers were notorious for the low wages they doled out to those working in the highly dangerous conditions in their works. In 1879, St Rollox paid a labourer (most of its workers were simply labourers) £40 a year (16/- a week) for a 60-hour week – about 3d (little more than 1p) an hour. In today's terms, this equates to about £1.50 an hour.

By this date, St Rollox employed 2,000 workers. A parliamentary enquiry into conditions in the alkali industry in the 1880s heard evidence from a trades union official named J. Mitchell, who claimed that floor sweepers at the alkali works on Tyneside, which were unionised, earned more than furnace labourers at St Rollox, who were not in a trades union. Tennant's (who also owned the Tyneside works) argued that cheaper coal on Tyneside was the cause of this wage difference. But the real reason was not cheaper coal – it was the abundant and never-ending supply of cheap labour on Clydeside – cheap labour that, in Tennant's case, was disproportionately Irish. The Garngad, like the Gorbals, became an early location for Irish immigration.

Garngad today rises above the M8 motorway. Thirty years ago, this motor route still carried the Monkland Canal, which was built to connect Glasgow to the coal and iron fields of Lanarkshire, but which was disused as a waterway from the 1960s. But the tale begins back in the 18th century in rural Ayrshire, with a man who signed Robert Burns's birth certificate – John Tennant. He was known as 'Auld Glen', from the farm he leased at a place called Glenconnor, and Burns thought highly of the man, later writing:

My heart's warm love to guid auld Glen
The ace and wale of honest men.

It was Auld Glen's son, Charles, who, after being apprenticed as a weaver at Kilbarchan was to establish the St Rollox Chemical Works on the canal in 1799 shortly after the opening of the waterway. Here, the bulk items of raw materials such as coal, lime and potash could be cheaply transported, and thence re-exported as bulk manufactured chemicals.

Charles Tennant's fortune was made by the industrial manufacture of bleaching powder, in a process which owed much to the chemical genius of his initial business partner Charles Macintosh. (The latter was a pioneer of scientific textile development, who was also to discover how to waterproof cotton by dissolving rubber with naptha, and thus give birth to waterproof clothing – hence the generic name 'Macintosh'.)

Bleaching powder soon replaced urine, sunlight and other inferior bleaches in the textile industry, and from this base the firm diversified into sulphuric acid, caustic soda and soap manufacture. By the time of his death in 1838, Charles Tennant employed 500 men, in what the *New Statistical Account* of the 1840s described as:

> ... This manufactory, the most extensive of any of the kind in Europe. In the furnaces are upwards of 100 furnaces, retorts and fire-places. In this great concern upwards of 600 tons of coal are consumed weekly.

This dependence on coal lead to Tennant's involvement in the promotion and financing of Scotland's first railway, the 1831 Glasgow and Garnkirk railway, which broke the Monkland canal company's monopoly over carriage of coal and chemicals, and which joined the coalfields of Lanarkshire to the St Rollox Chemical Works.

As one of the new industrial capitalist class, excluded from political power, Charles was a Radical, engaging in the struggle for political reform and abolition of the Corn Laws. One of the main reforming organisations at this time was the Crow Club, which grouped together many of Glasgow's leading businessmen and reformers. In *Glasgow and its Clubs*, John Strang tells us that Tennant gave his warehouse to be a meeting place of the Crow Club, and that 'Mr Charles Tennant was one of the leading members of the reform party in Glasgow'. Strang's chapter entitled 'Glasgow Politics in 1832 – Crow Club' is very interesting, not least in showing that he, like Tennant, approved of the agitation for middle-class reform, but disapproved of that by lower-class reformers. Charles, to give him his due, was 'radical' enough to refuse a peerage when it was offered to him shortly before his death. A life-size effigy in Carrara marble sits on top of his grave in Glasgow's Necropolis. Like other monuments here, it is much eroded – partly by the pollution produced by St Rollox, which lay less than half a mile away.

Even before the events of 1832, the year that saw the passing of the first Reform Act and the enfranchisement of the middle classes, Garngad had been a hotbed of radicalism. In 1816 a Glasgow businessman, James Turner, held a series of meetings for reform at Thrushgrove, his estate in the Garngad, which at that time lay mostly in open country.

Crowds of up to 40,000 people turned up at the meetings organised there. Later, as Garngad was built over, Turner (and Tennant) had streets named after them, and further ones were called after other Victorian bourgeois reformers, such as Cobden and Bright. The emerging working class supported these agitations enthusiastically, feeling that they too would benefit from them. Local trades unions turned out for the mass meeting on Glasgow Green of May 1832, attended by 120,000 people. Alas, when reform came in 1832, the working classes were excluded from its fruits.

Charles was followed by John Tennant, who expanded the firm's operations to Tyneside, where a factory even bigger than St Rollox was in existence from the 1860s (though with a smaller lum). At this time, the firm had a industrial near-monopoly in Britain, and was making money hand over fist. Part of the profits was used to diversify. As part of a wider consortium John acquired the Tharsis mines in Spain, where a Scottish colony of several hundred oversaw mining operations employing 2,000 people and producing iron ore, copper and sulphur. In 1866, with the products from these mines, John opened the Tharsis Sulphur and Copper Works in Garngad, where the mass use of cyanide added to the toxic mix of the area. This Tennant was a campaigner against the Corn Laws, and a stalwart of the Liberal Party in Glasgow, as were most of the rapacious capitalist industrial exploiters. But it was with Charles Tennant II that the dynasty was to reach its dizzy climax, and under whom the seeds of its ultimate collapse were sown.

Charles Tennant came into the firm's leadership in the 1870s, when Britain's industrial monopoly was just beginning to be challenged by the United States and Germany, with their much more scientific-based industrial practices. In 1884, he was forced to remain competitive by broadening the company's capital base and making it a public concern – Charles Tennant and Partners. However, Tennant's was producing caustic soda by the Leblanc process, one almost a century old, when overseas competitors were adopting the much more efficient (and less polluting) Solvay process. Tennant considered this option, but rejected it as it would mean an expensive re-equipping of his factories and consequent reduction in profits and dividends for an interim period. This rejection of scientific chemistry was an example of how, by 1900, Germany was able to dominate the world market in alkalis and other similar products.

Tennant's solution was partly to diversify into new areas. His venture into explosives, which he undertook with Nobel at Ardersier in Ayrshire, was a success, but that into steel production was not. He was, effectively, sacked as director of the Scottish Steel Company in 1895, when it was technically bankrupt. This company owned two works, Hallside in Lanarkshire and Blochairn on the east side of the Garngad, keeping up the local Tennant connection. Blochairn, too, was a notoriously polluting works. In fact, Tennant's Garngad connection goes further. The family owned much of the surrounding land, and made a great deal of money from the erection of poor-quality tenements in the area from the 1870s onwards. Garngad housing was bad – even by Glasgow standards. The houses generally had outside toilets, if toilets at all, and overcrowding was so great that the inspectors given the job of enforcing Glasgow's ticketing system (in which each room should have had a maximum number of occupants), noted that people were not only sleeping in the house lobbies but also on the stairs and closes of Garngad.

Charles Tennant's other policy was to keep wages to a rock-bottom low. In the Garngad he was able to do this in his factories with the availability of cheap, unskilled labour. But his Tyneside works were unionised, as was Hallside Steel Works, and he was not always able to pay wages as low as he would have liked. A visitor to the Tennant household in 1897 noted, 'my host is possessed by an almost maniacal hatred of trades unions and all their works'.

Tennant carried on the family tradition of political Liberalism, actually becoming Glasgow's MP from 1877–80, and serving for Peebles and Selkirk afterwards. But the political trajectory of the family clearly mirrors that of the British bourgeoisie in the 19th century, faced with the rise of foreign competition and of the labour movement: from radicalism to reaction. Free trade was the first of the Liberal policies to be abandoned. Competition was eliminated or reduced by amalgamations. Tennant merged with its main competitor in the soap industry, the Ogstons of Aberdeen, and also with its domestic rivals in bleach manufacturing, the United Alkali Company, in 1891. Although one of his daughters was to marry Asquith, a future Liberal prime minister, by his death in 1906 Tennant was a Conservative in all but name, supporting their policy of imposing import duties and serving on Chamberlain's Tariff Commission of 1904. He died with a fortune of over £3 million, a half-billionaire in today's terms.

Charles Tennant II had bought a country estate in Peeblesshire, which he called 'The Glen' after his ancestors' Ayrshire farm. He had divided his time between here and his house in London's Grosvenor Square, hardly ever visiting the outposts of his industrial empire. His son, who later became Lord Glenconnor – the full title of the original farm – lived the life of a country gentleman, and took little interest in the company, which by now was a public company not a family firm. Glenconnor dabbled in politics, spiritualism and philanthropy, giving a piece of waste ground in the Garngad to Glasgow Corporation, who subsequently turned it into Glenconnor Park. This shabby gift was the sum total of Tennant benefactions in Garngad.

Those who are interested in the further decline and fall of this paradigmatic capitalist family, whose firm eventually became absorbed into the I.C.I. empire, can read *Broken Blood* by Simon Blow. A better title for the book might have been 'The Sins of the Fathers'. One wonders what Auld Glen, the 'wale of men' would have made of these, his degenerate descendants. But enough of this (albeit necessary) account of the Tennants – let us go walkabout in the Garngad, known to the locals in their rhyming slang as 'The Good and the Bad'. Bad the Tennants certainly gave the Garngad and its inhabitants, in living, housing and working conditions. Any good the local people made themselves.

Garngad today

Today, the entire site of the St Rollox works has been cleared. The Stalk came down in the 1920s, and even then Tennants' legacy of death continued, when several men were killed in the demolition process. In addition, the canal, where the works had its own large berthing facilities at St Rollox basin, and the railway that ran through the works have also gone. Further, the region around is (for the pedestrian) the Gordian knot that is Junction 15 of the M8 motorway and the atrocity of the Expressway, which destroyed the railway metropolis of Springburn to the north of Garngad. But, standing on the M8 overpass at the north end of Castle Street, which formerly crossed the canal here and carried on northwards, you can see where the works once were: basically, they occupied the ground now bounded by Pinkston Road and Pinkston Drive, while the sports fields at Sighthill, and Sighthill Park itself were where the mounds of chemical waste were deposited. There are allotments here, but I wouldn't dig too deeply if one of them was mine.

The overpass becomes an underpass, and eventually leads you to Royston Road. After the slum clearance programmes of the 1930s, Glasgow Council went in for a bit of spin and decided to improve the image of the Garngad by renaming it, and all its applications, as Royston. You very quickly come to the first, and most successful, of these slum clearance programmes. Garngad Square was built in 1918–20, and consists of the first council houses constructed in Glasgow. It is still a well-maintained area, and has the honour that James Maxton, the MP for Bridgeton from 1922, lived here for a time. Garngad Square was built on the site of a cotton mill, which in the 19th century belonged to, one of Glasgow's provosts. In 1858 there was a strike, a 'turn out', here by 400 women workers when Galbraith brought in two technicians to double the amount of power looms each operative would work. The *Glasgow Sentinel* described the scene:

> At the meal hours these two men are escorted to their houses amidst the shouting and yelling not only of the hundreds of the 'turn outs' but by many of their sympathisers belonging to the factories and other public works in the same locality and notwithstanding the presence of Mr Galbraith and a posse of police... bills have been posted in the neighbourhood expressing 'Down with the nobs'.

The girls won their strike.

Just opposite Garngad Square is St Roch's (another name for St Rollox, who had a dedicated church hereabouts around 1500) Secondary School. Originally built in 1928, it was rebuilt after the Second World War and has recently undergone its Private Finance Initiative makeover. The school occupied the site of the former Glasgow Malleable Iron Works, where a boiler exploded in 1880, killing 17 people and injuring 35 – just another day in the Garngad. Almost nothing, except for one tenement on the south side of the street, remains on the now Royston Road to remind us of its 19th-century aspect; indeed, apart from a semi-derelict building showing faint signs of art deco further on, almost nothing remains of the social housing that replaced the tenements in the interwar period of the last century. The road has the appearance of a German city after the Second World War for much of its length, with gap sites, isolated buildings and a negative feel to the public domain.

The Royston Library is almost like a First World War pillbox; its lovely Edwardian predecessor, Townhead Library on Castle Street, was demolished for the M8 motorway and this is what the locals were given in return. Opposite, however, is an Edwardian survival. St Rollox Public School, built in 1906, is in a somewhat severe art nouveau style, and was designed by the firm of Duncan McNaughton. It is still in use as the local non-denominational primary, though a ghastly concrete entrance block from around the 1960s or 1970s has spoiled its bold frontage. In former outbuildings in the playground is the Rosemount Learning Centre, which provides a wide range of social and educational facilities for the area, and the courses of which are constantly over-subscribed. A couple of years ago, I led walks with Garngad women from Rosemount to various parts of Glasgow. Some amazed me with their knowledge, yet others had hardly stepped outside of the Garngad – not even to Springburn, across the railway line.

Most of my ladies stuck to the term Garngad, and so too does the last pub standing on 'Royston' Road, The Garngad Bar, another pillbox in its no-man's land. I was initially cheered at this sighting of a determination to maintain the area's nomenclatural heritage, and was taking a picture of the establishment when a local, half jokingly, nudged my elbow and advised, 'Dinnae go in there, son. That's a Celtic pub.'

How had I missed the obvious signs? No tricolour, no shamrock – but every door and window shutter painted green.

Immigrants have always been highly visible and their numbers exaggerated. This was the case in Glasgow – and Garngad – with the Irish, who were never, at any time, a majority in any principal area of the city, though they were in certain sub-localities. In 1851, for example, the Irish population of the Garngad was 25 per cent, and although it grew with time, they were never a majority. This can be compared with areas of Liverpool, where at the height of the Home Rule agitation an Irish nationalist MP was actually elected in that city. In the last census, 30 per cent of people in Garngad claimed nominal allegiance to Catholicism.

The Garngad has retained a Catholic sub-identity in a similar but stonger way to the Gorbals. As well as the pub, the local secondary school is a Catholic one, and at the end of Royston Road, before one

ST ROLLOX AND CATHEDRAL, SULEMAN ENGRAVING, 1864
The lum of the works can be seen less than half a mile from Scotland's finest medieval
cathedral – and Glasgow's main hospital

comes to Glenconnor Park, is a Catholic complex consisting of St Roch's Primary School (founded in 1907), a church and a Catholic mission. And in some of the houses you will see the occasional tricolour flag that conveys not only a footballing allegiance but an explicitly stated political one as well. That sectarianism in the working class has been a problem here cannot be denied. In the 1930s, the Garngad was a not infrequent scene of sectarian rioting around Orange and Hibernian parades, and in 1925 even firearms were used in a riot following an Orange march. But here, as elsewhere, the events around the First World War (and the subsequent partial settling of the Irish question) changed things. In 1912 the Labour Party did not even put up a candidate in St Rollox, so dominated was that election by the Irish Home Rule crisis. In 1922, the same party took the seat in a landslide, with almost 60 per cent of the vote.

Most of the Garngad's industry lay in a line from the St Rollox works to the present Glenconnor Park, along the dual axes of Garngad Street and Charles Street. The chemical works were the biggest, and employed mainly Irish immigrants. Much of the other industry was also unskilled, including the cotton mill, which employed female labour, and a couple of foundries. There were exceptions. In 1907, Cowieson's built a factory for the construction of prefabricated steel buildings, and diversified into bodies for buses. There was also a small clay pipe factory,

Glasgow's last, which, incredibly closed in 1967. Was anyone using clay pipes in the 1960s? Most of the sites of these former works, around Charles Street, have become a modern trading estate.

At Tharsis Street, named after Tennant's mines in Spain, we come to a still-functioning relic of the past, the Foundry Boys' Church. The Glasgow Foundry Boys' Religious Society was established in the 19th century as an offshoot of Victorian evangelicalism, to spread the gospel, and social welfare, among the workers of Glasgow's many iron foundries. Originally located elsewhere (and known as the Protestant Foundry Boys), the church moved to Tharsis Street in 1894, and is still functioning today, though not a foundry boy (or man) remains in the city. This was a very active organisation, which regularly took 1,000 kids on a summer outing before the First World War, and was still carrying out charitable and religious work in the 1960s. Such an organisation would develop other functions. Clearly, those parents who supported the group and sent their children to the church would stand in better stead with foremen and managers of local businesses than those who did not, leading to the possibility of preferential treatment for employment and promotion. And it got your kids off your hands for a while as well, which for most people was the main thing.

Next we come to the Copperworks, some excellent modern co-ownership and housing association tenemented properties, which are typical of the kind of housing being constructed all over the Garngad. The Copperworks was built on the site of the Tharsis factory, and Micheal Keenan, in his book *Garngad* (a typewritten copy is in Royston Library), mentions the piles of copper slag, called 'Blue Billy' here when he was a boy. Keenan thought it had something to do with William of Orange. Keenan's memoir is a warm and touching account of the Garngad from the 1920s to the present day, covering religion, housing, social life and sport. If his account is an accurate reflection of life there, the Garngad was not a political place: not once does he mention politics: no elections, no strikes, no political activists.

In the last 20 years, the Garngad has been rebuilt for the third time, and this time it looks like having more chance of success. There is a mix of rented, co-ownership and affordable private housing in the area, and it appears that, unlike the New Gorbals, most of the people living here have been relocated from the previous housing, thus maintaining community links.

The improvement of housing requires the associated improvement of public space and sadly so far, that is lacking in the Garngad. Public facilities such as libraries and schools need to present a positive outlook, shops and pubs need to be attractive, and rubbish needs to be cleared.

At the eastern reaches of Garngad, where it is divided from Germiston by the railway, we come to Glenconnor Park, the only green space available for a long way around for the Garngad people. The state of this park, with its undermaintained sports fields and derelict bowling green, is a disgrace. But the squeaky axle gets the grease, and sadly, in places like Garngad, people do not have a culture of complaint nor the skills to apply political pressure, unlike the middle classes of the city.

From Glenconnor Park, it is a steep walk uphill along Roystonhill (formerly Garngad Hill). From here you can see where the St Rollox Works stood to the west, and its Tharsis offshoot to the north, and you also overlook the site of the former Blochairn Steel Works, now Glasgow's Fruit Market, lying south-easterly.

Here stands the lonely steeple of Townhead and Blochairn Church, which was rescued, unlike the demolished church itself, by Glasgow Buildings Preservation Trust. It was a small community garden. Again, maintenance is as important as creation, and the garden now suffers from neglect and was locked on my last couple of visits. From here, the view must be the best in Glasgow: Tinto to the south, Arran to the west and the Campsies to the north. Changed days from those when a cartoon could be published showing nothing but blackness and chimneys, entitled 'A Clear Day at St Rollox'.

The brick and render three-storey tenements of Glasgow Corporation were built on Garngad Hill, and

A CLEAR DAY AT ST ROLLOX
Pollution became a byword in Victorian Britain, provoking this sardonic comment

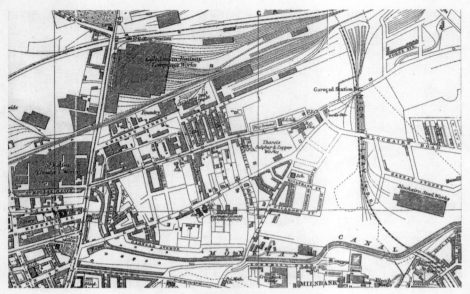

MAP OF GARNGAD IN 1908
This shows the huge concentration of polluting industries
surrounding the working-class housing

were a social disaster – unlike much of their other slum clearance programmes in the 1920s and 1930s. Most of these are gone now and have
been replaced by the much more visually attractive architectural styles of
the 1980s and 1990s. Indeed, you might say that after 200 years, the
people of the Garngad have finally achieved housing conditions that are
fit for human beings. Its population is rising after 50 years of decline,
with the arrival of economic migrants from Eastern Europe, asylum
seekers from Africa and refugees from Iraq, devastated by the Blair–Bush
'liberation'. What the population now needs is for their public spaces to be
upgraded and – of course, much harder to provide locally in today's free
market, globalised economy – they need work. But for all that, there are
worse places in Glasgow today than the Garngad, and that is not something that could have easily been said in the past. Despite the over-
reaching spire dominating Garngad Hill, it is not heaven – but no longer
is it a living hell redeemed only by the enormous capacity of its population
for endurance.

CHAPTER 7

Cathcart:
Red Clyde Tributary

AT FIRST, CATHCART is not a district you might associate with important aspects of working-class history. The last three-quarters of a century have seen the surrounding areas on either side of the White Cart River disappear under mushroom fields of middle-class suburbia. In the 1880s, the railway reached Cathcart and suburbanisation began even then. The classic image of the bourgeoisie at play, Lavery's *The Tennis Party* was painted in Cartbank Villa in Cathcart in the Edwardian era – though, truth be told, Cartbank was an 18th century mansion. However, for a time it was uncertain whether Cathcart would become an industrial satellite of Glasgow or the residential suburb it ended up as.

Cathcart was annexed to Glasgow in 1912. Previously, it had been a small village with a couple of paper-making factories, a carpet-weaving works and a few smaller industries, with a scattering of coal pits and quarries. In 1913, a large textile works, the Wallace Scott Tailoring Institute, was erected in Cathcart. Beside this stood what was to be the main employer in the area for over a century, Weir's Pumps, which was established in 1886 and employed 3,000 workers at the time of annexation.

The radicalisation of Weir's workers – and others locally – by the events of the First World War was shown by the General Election of 1922. Cathcart narrowly elected J.P. Hay, one of the 10 left-wing MPs from Glasgow belonging to the Independent Labour Party (ILP) which had opposed (or rather, not supported) the war, and which demanded the nationalisation of the basic industries. Coming after the bitter strikes at Weir's during the war itself, this election must have had suburban Cathcart quaking in its tennis shoes.

As with many other areas, the boundaries of Cathcart are a topic that generates intense debate. For me, Cathcart is defined by the aspects of its history that I want to discuss, but it is as well to start from an indisputable point – Cathcart station on the famous Cathcart Circle line.

This railway route probably determined that the area would – eventually – become predominantly middle class rather than working class. Between the wars of the last century, the population of Cathcart was almost doubled by private residential developments.

Delvin Road takes you across the Cart and a right turn along Castle Road leads to the charmingly named Snuff Mill Road, and the old Cathcart Bridge, which carried the main road from Cathcart to Glasgow for 300 years until its closure in 1924. Those who know William 'Crimea' Simpson's delightful collection of watercolours, *Glasgow in the 1840s*, will recognise the scene, changed though it has since 1845, the 'thackit hooses' having been demolished. This was a favourite spot for walkers from the city, who came to view the now-demolished Cathcart Castle, and MacDonald, in his *Rambles Round Glasgow* (1854), stated that it had two inns:

> one of which, that of Mr Mitchell, is an exceedingly neat and comfortable place of rest and refreshment. [His] garden plot with its flower beds and bee hives is a perfect model of neatness and beauty.

Sneaking into view behind the bridge in Simpson's painting is the lum of the old snuff mill. This was actually a paper mill, and snuff manufacture was a small sideline. The works was established by Solomon Lindsay in 1812 and operated for almost a century. The Lindsays were hardly pioneers of the new industrial age. The mill never employed more than 20 workers, with a safe niche at the quality end of the paper market, and was unmechanised for most of its existence. The Lindsays and their sons laboured alongside their workers in an almost pre-industrial, merchant capitalist fashion.

David Lindsay, the second of the line, appeared to have had fleeting ambitions of a sort. He leased the land for his mill from the Earl of Cathcart and asked for permission to erect a house, as he intended to marry. With this permission, once granted in 1863, he constructed Lindsay House, which still stands by the bridge. When the laird saw the building, he commented, 'I gave you permission to build a cottage, but you have built a palace.' Abashed, the timorous Davie not only remained in his previous modest cottage and sub-let Lindsay House as tenement dwellings, but he also cancelled his marriage. Clearly, the Lindsays were

NEW LANARK MILLS, c.1800
Owen's social experiment, in its idyllic setting, became a 'must-see' for the
middle- and upper-class tourist. Some can be seen on horseback

NEW LANARK SCHOOL 1818
Owen enlisted music, dance and visual stimuli for his educational purposes
– and banned corporal punishment

DALZELL PLATE MILLS, MOTHERWELL
The fine office building of the only remaining steel plant in the former 'Steelopolis'

MOTHERWELL BRIDGE
The futuristic cooling
towers loom over a
much reduced fabrication
facility

PROVAN HALL AND BLOCHAIRN HOUSE
The additions to the 15th century mansion were built with money from
slave plantations

THE FORT, EASTERHOUSE
Titanium Shopping Cathedral. Eighty per cent of the jobs have been taken
up by local people

HOUSING, EASTERHOUSE 1950s
Much of this is now being demolished

HOUSING, EASTERHOUSE 2000s
A great improvement – and it's a 50s renovation, not a new build

1930s HOUSING, GARNGAD
Look hard, there are a few Art Deco touches. Local patriotism is shown
by the continued use of the real name for the area

2000s HOUSING, GARNGAD
Excellent housing – Co-operative flats on the former Copperworks site

TAILORING WORKS, CATHCART
No Satanic Mill but a masterpiece of industrial architecture,
now the headquarters of Scottish Power

WIER'S PUMPS, CATHCART
The above's neighbour, another splendid piece of industrial design.
Hopefully proposed conversion to housing will retain, not destroy it

COUNCIL HOUSING, CATHCART
Magnificent tenement-style housing, with gardens, balconies

SCOTLAND STREET SCHOOL, KINNING PARK
One of Charles Rennie Mackintosh's masterpieces, now an Education Museum

THE SCWS HEADQUARTERS, KINGSTON
A monument to the initial success of the Co-operative Movement, and (now flats and offices) to its later failure

SCOTTISH SOCIALIST PARTY OFFICES, KINNING PARK
Colourful agit-prop murals. Will they last? – Party troubles mean the offices were recently put up for sale

WEAVERS COTTAGES, PAISLEY
From such howffs came cloth, poetry, and radical politics

CLARK'S ANCHOR THREAD MILLS, PAISLEY
Once one of the biggest cotton mills in the world, now flats and offices

'COMET' 1962 REPLICA,
PORT GLASGOW
The former shipyard itself is now
another Tescotown

FERGUSON'S SHIPYARD, PORT GLASGOW
Still – just – holding on as the last merchant shipbuilder on the Clyde

JAMES WATT STATUE,
GREENOCK
Beside his birthplace in
the town

SUGAR WAREHOUSES, GREENOCK
This UNESCO-Listed building is a beauty in brick. Currently being weatherproofed and
stabilised, and awaiting future use

TOWN HALL, GREENOCK
Possibly not as opulent as
Glasgow City Chambers, but
a more graceful building
nevertheless

CRANES AT DRY DOCK,
GREENOCK
The nearby Arrol 'Goliath' crane
was sadly demolished, but here
are a couple of the last working
cranes on the Clyde, at a ship
repair facility

HIRAM WALKERS TOWER,
DUMBARTON
All that remains of the
distillery built in the 1930s
to supply Prohibition
America with hooch.
It was the biggest grain
distillery in the world

SHIPYARD WORKERS, GREENOCK
A fine memorial to the men who built ships in the town for almost 200 years, and a
group of youngsters a couple generations down the de-industrialisation road

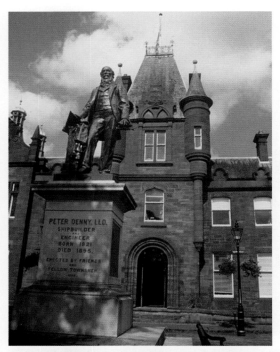

DENNY STATUE, DUMBARTON
One of the shipbuilding clan
outside the former Town Hall

DENNY SHIP TANK
The first non military one in the world, in use until the 1980s, now part of the
Scottish Maritime Museum

MURAL, WOMEN'S INSTITUTE, ALEXANDRIA
Showing the 'Duties of Women' (childrearing, housekeeping, etc.). At that time,
however, the Turkey Red Capitalists worked their female workers 60 hours a week in
the mills, preventing them from carrying out any of these duties

STRATHLEVEN HOUSE, THE VALE
Palladian mansion, later home of Turkey Red industrial dynasty

ARGYLL MOTOR WORKS,
ALEXANDRIA
Of all the industrial places and
fabulous factories, this has to be
the greatest; inside is as opulent
as outside. Now a retail outlet

HOUSING, ENGELS STREET, 1930s
Splendid cottage-style flats, built
when the Vale was 'Red'. We
started with Owen, we end with
Engels. Socialism – Utopian and
Scientific?

not the material of a new bourgeoisie world order. The mill buildings have today been converted to dwellings in what remains one of the most charming spots in the city.

If the Lindsays looked backwards to the handicraft age, there was another paper mill on the Cart that expressed some of the realities of the Victorian industrial era more truly. Alongside the rapacious exploitation that most Victorian employers practised was a tradition – sometimes religiously inspired – of paternalism in the workplace. The Couper brothers of Cathcart are a classic example of this. Crossing the old bridge on the Cart, and taking the riverside walkway to the foot of Millholm Road, leads to both the site of their factory and thence to the still-standing Holmwood House, built by one of the Couper brothers in parkland above the bend in the Cart lying below. When here I like to take the long way to these sites, staying on the east side of the Cart and walking through the fine Linn Park, before crossing back to the west side just south of Cathcart cemetery, by the arching cast iron bridge (one of the first constructed in the Glasgow area) and then following the river northwards downstream. The former Cathcart Castle, the ruins of which I recall from three decades ago, is now gone, though the mansion house in the park, Linn House, has been saved from its former dereliction by its conversion into flats.

Paper-making was begun on the Cart by a French Huguenot refugee, Nicholas Deschamp, who both invested in the Darien Scheme in 1696 and supplied paper to the Darien Company. It seems likely that his descendants were involved in the establishment of the paper mill at Millholm, which was leased by the Couper brothers from 1841 and then bought by them in 1853. The year was important, for the Crimean war had broken out and the Coupers obtained a large contract to supply the government with paper; three years later, by the end of the war, they had made a substantial amount of money. Government work and legal contracts made up the bulk of their work thenceforth.

Quality rather than price was the key to government contracts. The Stationery Office set up shops to sell the paper it bought that was not up to required quality, but there was little of the Coupers' production among this. When they bought the factory, all paper was hand made, and though they mechanised it, the mill remained water powered throughout most of their occupancy, a steam engine being installed a few years before the mill was sold in 1884. The mill ran under a variety of owners, including Wiggin's Teape, until it finally closed in 1929 and was demolished in 1938. Devotees of industrial archaeology can still enjoy investigating the ruins of the mill, including the overgrown lade, at the foot of Millholm Road.

The Coupers were first-generation capitalists, working men who had taken advantage of the opportunities available at the time. The size of their workplace remained medium scale, with between 200 and 300 workers, and its market was insulated from fierce competition. These were ideal conditions for the practise of paternalistic relations, and – even allowing for the habit of not speaking ill of the dead – commentators generally observe that the Coupers were 'model' employers. In his *Memories of Cathcart* (1938), Alexander Gartshore says of the Coupers:

> They were men of sterling quality and principle, assiduous in their business, invariably being found at their post whether in the office or the mill. They interested themselves in the welfare of their workers, in cases of illness paying their wages in full.

When Robert Couper died in 1883 he left money in his will to give his workers a lump sum, on a sliding scale according to how long they had worked in the mill, and also funds to supply the workers with a paid holiday. He also left money to be allocated for the relief 'of the deserving poor of Cathcart', and a sum of £8,500 for the establishment of 'a hall, with a Library and a reading room' in Cathcart. Though the mill is long gone, the Couper Institute in Clarkston Road, built to designs by James Sellars in 1887–8, still stands as a monument to Victorian paternalistic capitalism. Dropping down Netherlee Road from Holmwood House takes you via Rhannan Road to Clarkston Road, where the Couper Institute, now the local library, stands. It is an interesting building but this is not the main contribution the brothers made to the architectural legacy of the city.

The Crimean War had enriched the siblings. Robert commissioned James Smith – father of Madeleine Smith – to build him a villa, Sunnyside, on land just above the factory in the mid 1850s. Smith was possibly preoccupied at this time with the cause célèbre of his daughter, accused (but acquitted Not Proven) of murdering her French lover, and Sunnyside was a poor example of his work, subsequently demolished in

HOLMWOOD VILLA
Alexander 'Greek' Thomson's villa quickly achieved iconic status

the 1960s. James, on the other hand, chose Alexander Thomson to build him a house adjacent to Sunnyside, and this turned out to be probably Thomson's finest villa, Holmwood. From his front porch it took Couper a brisk three-minute walk to the gates of his factory below – 'living above the shop' indeed. Today, Holmwood House is operated and owned by the National Trust for Scotland and is becoming, with restoration, an increasingly intact example of Thomson's genius. Included in the stunning interior are 21 illustrations to Homer's *Iliad*. One can only appreciate this architectural masterpiece by seeing it.

At the time of Robert Couper's death, Cathcart was still a small industrial village of about 3,000 people, as described by Gartshore:

> At that time the majority of the inhabitants of the village of Cathcart were employed in the two paper mills – Couper's and Lindsay's – and in the dye works and carpet factory owned by the two brothers, William and John Geddes.

By the time of annexation by Glasgow in 1912, the population had increased five-fold – the reasons were two events of 1886. The Cathcart Circle railway came to the village, and with it suburbanisation, and so too did the firm of Weir's pumps, whose rapid expansion in the next three decades led to the construction of tenemented dwellings for its work-force along Holmlea Road and the surrounding area.

James Weir came of farming stock from Airdrie, but trained as a pro-fessional engineer in Fairfield's shipyard in Govan, where John Elder had just patented the compound steam engine, revolutionising shipbuilding construction. James was a highly talented engineer. Engines needed pumps, and he designed ones for recycling waste-water boiler heat and also solved problems with the corrosion of boilers caused by salt water. He initially contracted out the manufacturing of pumps for marine engineering, then set up, with his brother, J. & G. Weir's at Cathcart in 1886, with 14 men. The market was limitless, and whenever new developments came, Weir was first. He pioneered pumps for oil when this began to replace coal in ships, and was at the forefront of the application of electricity to marine pump technology.

Weir's built the best marine pumps in the world, and by 1914 the navies of most nations – including Germany – stipulated that only Weirs' pumps should be in their ships. By 1895, Weir's had 900 workers and by 1913, there were 3,000 skilled engineers working at Cathcart. These men were members of the Amalgamated Society of Engineers (ASE), one of the best organised craft unions in the country. In 1897–8, the ASE launched a strike for the eight-hour day, but this was defeated by the employers, and in its aftermath the craft privileges of the engineers were reduced. Weir retired in 1910 and left £560,000 in his will, the equivalent of about £50–60 million in today's money.

James's son, William, entered the firm and became a director in 1902. A visit to the United States in 1901 convinced William that the times were a-changing and that 'Americanisation' represented the way of the future. He was impressed by the 'scientific management' has saw practised in the United States and became an advocate of work study, standardisation and payment by results, all of which contradicted British industrial practice. William Weir was so impressed by the United States that when he engaged in a major expansion of the Cathcart works in 1912–13, he bought a modernisitic ferro-concrete design from the American architect Albert Kahn, builder of many US industrial plants.

Northwards from the Couper Institute, Newlands Road leads west to the factory. The factory is a splendid building, but Weir was to find that imitating US industrial architecture was easier than importing US industrial relations. The ASE had recovered from the disastrous strike defeat of 1898, and in the pre-war industrial boom was able to both advance wages and maintain good working conditions.

Harry McShane trained as an engineer before the First World War, and moved with apparent ease from factory to factory in a deliberate policy of widening his industrial experience and training. He worked for most of 1914 in Weir's and left us with interesting observations on the place. With other commentators, he agreed that Weir's was the best organised factory in Glasgow:

> In Weir's in 1914 there was a real factory committee in operation. The secretary of the committee was James Messer, a member of the ILP [Independent Labour Party], and every week all the shop stewards met and discussed the affairs of the factory.

McShane led a strike in his section of the works for the reinstatement of a shop steward, and describes, in his book *No Mean Fighter*, what followed:

> I got all my men ready and we walked out through the works. The men on the benches rattled their hammers all the way along as a way of applauding. They all came out on strike that evening.

The 'Americanisation' of work at Weir's had led to its sub-division. McShane had been used to highly skilled work in machine building and in the shipyards, and commented that at Weir's:

> each man knew what job he was going to do during the day. The jobs were so ridiculously simple that anyone could do them.

And the introduction of piece-work, in such a well-organised works, meant that the ASE had been able to push up piece-rates:

> ... everything in Weir's was on bonus. It meant we got £1 a week more, but I don't remember anyone having to rush for it.

William Weir felt that the war presented him with his opportunity to destroy this shop-floor organisation. He himself was to be one of those 'hard-faced men who did well out of the war' – during the conflict the capitalisation of his firm doubled. Like many others, he made huge amounts of money manufacturing munitions for the government at a 'no questions asked' cost of production, plus 10 per cent profit. However, he was infuriated that the workers were not satisfied with patriotic speeches, commenting:

> The skilled workmen have clearly demonstrated their inability to resist the temptations offered to them by the shortage of men. The proof of this is shown by excessive wage claims, by the enforcement of restrictions on production, by bad time keeping and by drink.

In 1915, Weir's saw the first major strike during the First World War. The company had withheld a two-pence-an-hour increase granted to the ASE before the conflict had broken out, and then Weir's imported engineers from the United States at a higher rate of pay to meet the labour shortage caused by the war. A strike by their 3,000 workers quickly spread to several other munitions works in Glasgow, and Weir's was forced to give in to some of the workers' demands.

The strike was to leave Weir with an abiding and lifelong hatred of trades unionism, and also a more immediate desire to be avenged, an opportunity that came his way when he joined the Ministry of Munitions in 1915, giving up direct management of Weirs – though he remained a director for another four decades. The Weir's strike had led to the formation of the Clyde Workers' Committee (CWC), a strange alliance of craft unionists intent on resisting dilution of their conditions of labour, and their shop steward leaders, often inspired by opposition to the war itself and the vision of a new socialist society.

It is no exaggeration to say that the outcome of the war depended on the introduction of dilution into the engineering trades, and that the Clyde, with its huge concentration of workers – almost 250,000 – working on munitions was in turn the key to this. Lloyd George realised the defeat of German imperialism by British imperialism depended on this battle more than on any in the trenches of France. So, too, did Weir, whose name hardly crops up in the official histories of the 'Dilution Crisis' of 1916. But W. J. Reader's book, *Architect of Airpower: A Life of Viscount Weir* shows from Weir's own and other papers that he was the driving force behind the vacillating Lloyd George's use of the draconian powers of the Defence of the Realm Act to arrest CWC leaders, deport them, suppress newspapers such as *Forward*, and in the last resort be prepared to use troops to shoot down strikers if necessary. This proved unnecessary, as David Kirkwood at Parkhead Forge did a private deal with William Beardmore, the owner of Parkhead Forge, which broke the back of the CWC's anti-dilution struggle.

After the war, Weir played little part in running the firm that bore his name, and of which he was chairman, and entered politics in the House of Lords. His last intervention at Cathcart was to try and persuade the Associated Ironmoulders' Union at the Cathcart foundry to de-skill their work and allow it to be done by semi-skilled workers, arguing that they did 'no work which cannot be carried out by a man or woman of ordinary intelligence after six weeks' training'. The Ironmoulders sucessfully resisted this, as too did the building trades unions, when Weir set up factories in the 1920s to mass produce prefabricated housing, using unskilled labour both in parts fabrication and on-site assembly. Interestingly, John Wheatley, the ILP Housing Minister in the brief Labour Government of 1923–4, was interested in Weir's mass production housing schemes, but demurred when he discovered Weir's anti-trades union agenda.

Weir was more successful in his class-warrior role in the corridors of power, as the man behind the scenes and one of the main policy-makers in the Conservative party between the wars, for which services he was made a Viscount in 1938. He was on the boards of ICI, Lloyd's Bank and, for a time, he was President of the British Employers' Federation. He had an influence on the crafting of the Trades Disputes Act of 1927, which outlawed general and sympathy strikes after the defeat of the General Strike in 1926. In the House of Lords, he described the unions as:

> ... tools of the extremist... the forcing houses of class warfare... the avowed aim of many of their officials is the overthrow of the existing structure of society.

His fingerprints are also to be found on the measures that were drawn up by the MacDonald Labour government in 1931, which cut unemployment benefit, civil servants' pay and social expenditure generally.

But his main influence on policy was probably in helping to persuade the governments of the 1930s to abandon free trade, arguing that what was needed was 'less of internationalism and much more of imperialism'. This policy led to the imposition of import duties on a wide range of goods. Weir was a firm advocate of the free market – but not for workers in trades unions to use to raise their wages, and certainly not if the free market would result in the ruination of British industry in the crisis of the 1930s.

Weir's Pumps survived the 1930s depression, largely based on the market for pumps created by re-armament, of which Weir was an influential advocate. From 1946 it was no longer a family firm – the company expanded in the post-war years to become a medium-sized multinational, one of British capitalism's success stories, developing markets in oil, power generation and desalination equipment. They survived the 1980s recession by buying and closing their main rival, Mather and Platt of Manchester, but the Cathcart works became a decreasing part of Weir's operations, and was down to 600 workers by the beginning of the 21st century.

Cathcart's 600 workers were producing an annual profit of £6 million in the early part of this decade. At a rough wage of £20,000 per worker, that represents a profit of £10,000 per employee per year; or, in Marxist terms, a rate of exploitation of 50 per cent – not bad going. But, going back on a previous commitment to relocate the works to a green-field site and retain the workforce, Weir's announced in 2006 that their Cathcart site would close. The plan was to dispose of the site for housing, and to sell the firm's intellectual capital to Weir's main industrial rival, Sultzer of Switzerland. This deal would net Weir's £100 million – amounting to over 15 years' profit at Cathcart at the stroke of a pen, and resulting in the loss of 600 highly skilled jobs. The first part of the deal went through, but the second faltered and eventually Weir's were forced to sell the pumps division as a going concern.

Another ground-breaking local factory has not fared so well. The Wallace Scott Tailoring Institute stood beside Weir's and was built to designs by J. J. Burnett in 1913. This was a revolutionary design in glass, steel and polychrome brick, but was also a garden factory, with sports grounds and a garden for the workers, as well as good internal facilities, including baths, showers and a dining hall. The tailoring works was closed in the 1950s and became the headquarters of the South of Scotland Electricity Board, later Scottish Power, who have car- parked the former gardens and made several brutal intrusions into the building itself.

With around 1,500 workers, this operations centre and call centre is the largest employer in the area today, and one of the largest in Glasgow. Since privatisation, Scottish Power has itself become a rapacious multinational, and its Cathcart base has seen frequent industrial disputes concerning its white-collar and highly unionised workforce. Despite being turned into a huge car park, elements of the garden remain and make it possibly one of the most scenic car parks in the world. Wandering through the gardened car park brings you to a pedestrian footbridge across the Cart and into Gryffe Street.

Here, on Holmlea Road and the surrounding streets, are the tenements built for the workers who came to Weir's in the late 19th century. Some of them are of high quality and remain, but others were less good and several have been demolished and replaced by some of the better social housing built by Glasgow Corporation in the inter-war period. Indeed, some of the three-storey tenements in red sandstone constructed around Gryffe Street must rank among the best social housing to be found anywhere in the UK. Why could they not all have been like this?

Walking back down Holmlea Street takes you to Cathcart station again, but if we stretch the boundaries of Cathcart just a little, a walk along Battlefield Road to the Battlefield Rest leads to what must be the finest former tram (later bus) shelter and kiosk in creation. Threatened with demolition in the 1980s, it has found a life-giving reinvention. The delightfully tiled building, with its copper ogee roof, is now an Italian restaurant, and well worth not missing as a place at which to end a ramble round Cathcart. A perambulation today is very different from that enjoyed by pedestrians such as MacDonald in the 1850s, but just as interesting.

There are strange ironies which lurk in events. As Scottish Conservatism near collapsed in the 1980s with the advent of a Thatcherism out of tune with Scottish middle-class values, Cathcart remained one of the only two Glasgow constituencies that returned Tory MPs. However, the inclusion of the post-war housing estate of Castlemilk within its boundaries made the seat a marginal one. Teddy Taylor, the brylcreamed heart-throb of Cathcart matrons, decided to give up the constituency he had held for many years and fled to a safe Tory seat on the English south coast. After 60 years, Cathcart returned a Labour MP: John Maxton. He was a descendant of the firebrand James, but without the fire in his forebear's belly.

CHAPTER 8

Atlantis:
Kingston and Kinning Park

HAD I BEEN Hugh MacDonald writing this chapter for a follow-up to his *Rambles Round Glasgow* – a sequel which sadly never transpired – I would doubtless have called it *'Twixt Gorbals and Govan* in the prolix style of the Victorians. MacDonald would have described the many fine rural mansions of the Glasgow bourgeoisie which stood here and he would also have annotated the local scenery with his fund of historical lore. The world that MacDonald knew when he walked hereabouts between 1830 and 1850 has absolutely vanished. And almost vanished also, has the world which replaced it; that of an industrial burgh of brief life, Kinning Park, and of the Glasgow suburb of Kingston, though these have disappeared not quite so completely. However, a little of this proletarian Atlantis is still visible below the waves of traffic on the M8 motorway.

Glasgow is the only British city through which a multi-lane motorway runs. Even when it was widely realised that this was the world's finest Victorian city, the idea was that most of it would be demolished. The infamous Bruce Plan, following the Second World War, envisaged not only the obliteration of all of the city's tenement dwellings, but also the replacement of the Victorian and Georgian city centre with modernist concrete buildings. Motorway construction would be the artery of this new urbanism. Even though this plan was heavily watered down (largely for reasons of cost rather than of aesthetics or social cohesion) in the 'comprehensive redevelopment' of the 1960s and 1970s, much that was of architectural and social value was demolished along with the slum dwellings that were necessarily flattened. Anderston, to the north of the River Clyde, and the composite district of Kingston–Tradeston–Kinning Park to the south were probably the areas which suffered most, as the motorway was driven directly through them.

The year 2006 witnessed the centenary of the construction of one of the masterpieces by Scotland's greatest architect, Charles Rennie

NEW QUAY, SIMPSON PRINT
Shows the construction of Kingston Dock on the site of the former Todd
and MacGregor shipyard

Mackintosh. Scotland Street School was completed by Glasgow School Board in 1906 as the main primary school for the areas of Kingston and Tradeston, which lie between the Gorbals to the east and Govan to the west, on the south bank of the Clyde.

Glasgow schools of this time were built to a high standard, but also to a fairly standard design. Mackintosh varied the format in Scotland Street by adding Scots baronial tower staircases, thus flooding the building with light. To the then normal provision of separate boys' and girls' entrance doors (and of course, separate playgrounds), Mackintosh added a diminutive door for infants. All the decorative features, such as ironwork and tiling, received the distinctive Mackintosh touch. This involved the architect in constant battles with the school board, whose misgivings were confirmed when Mackintosh spent £1,500 over budget. The total cost for the building was £34,291. It was once the local jewel in the crown, now the A-listed building is more like an oasis in a desert.

Scotland Street School was designed for a school roll of 1,250 pupils in a thriving community, but the school now stands marooned in one of those dead areas so typically produced by the redevelopment of our cities in the last 40 years. It is surrounded by trading estates and brown sites, and separated from the remaining pockets of population in the vicinity by the barrier of the M8 motorway. Such redevelopment and road building shattered and swept away many communities lying between Govan and the Gorbals. It is hard to credit that Kingston and Tradeston, with neighbouring Kinning Park, were populous enough in 1906 to form the parliamentary constituency of Tradeston, which lasted until the 1950s. However, by around 1980 the population of both Kingston and Tradeston in particular must have been heading towards absolute zero.

Mackintosh's school was closed in 1979, at a time when inner cities were seen as potential motorways and trading estates, with no future as centres of population. By that time its roll had fallen to less than 100. It now exists as Glasgow's Museum of Education, where today's children can role-play the history of education in various classrooms, set out as they were in the Victorian era, and through the inter-war period, to the 1950s and 1960s. Adults who pay the school the worthwhile visit should add to their enjoyment by taking a look at what is left of the community it served for three-quarters of a century: after more than four decades of decline and decay, there are encouraging signs of improvement.

It is easy to get to Scotland Street School: the subway station at Shields Road is just across the road. This had been open for less than 10 years by the time the school was built, and it gave locals quick access to the city centre and to the bustling shipyards of Govan to the west, where many worked. Doubtless, they were as proud of their new subway as they were of their fine new school building. And this is something we can easily forget about in areas such as Kingston: a century ago, they were brand-new areas, growing at a great rate, over land that within recent memory had been green countryside, or the site of fine mansions such as Plantation House and Cessnock House.

Would that the City Faithers, who had constructed Britain's second underground for the Second City, had been far sighted enough to make this transport system much more extensive. Then we might have been spared some of what we see around Shields Road. The coherent grid street plan existing in 1906, which connected the school and its environs to the rest of Kingston and to neighbouring Kinning Park, has been obliterated by flyovers and slipways of the M8, leaving pockets, including the school, trapped between the motorway and the railway lines to the south, which formerly separated Kingston and Kinning Park from Pollokshields. One consolation was that from the M8 one could have a splendid view of Mackintosh's school, especially when lit by night. Now a multi-storey park-and-ride facility for the subway has been built, blocking out any view of the school. Planning is improving, but dreadful, and avoidable, mistakes such as this continue to be made. Would Barcelona block off a Gaudi building from sight, with a car park?

Kingston was still expanding in 1906, with streets of grid-plan tenements being erected. Hereabouts, the area was one of the better in terms of housing, certainly superior to the neighbouring Gorbals. The workers in Kingston and Tradeston (and Kinning Park) were mainly skilled, with engineering predominating. Just next door to Scotland Street School can still be seen the façade of Howden's engineering works, awaiting future use – or demolition. At its height, Howden's employed more than 2,000 men making heavy engineering equipment. The works surrounded Scotland Street School on three sides, and apparently the weans would often jump the school wall to play in the works. Many of them would eventually 'cross the wall' more permanently to take employment in Howden's.

Harry McShane was born in Tradeston and started his apprenticeship as an engineer in Howden's. Here he first met socialists – members of the Social Democratic Federation and the Independent Labour Party (ILP), such as Willie Booth, who McShane described as 'an exceptional man because most workmen were either Liberals or Tories. In Glasgow the majority were Liberal'. Here, too, McShane engaged in his first industrial action, a strike of apprentices. He was sacked just after finishing his time, when refusing to scab during another apprentices' strike. McShane then moved to the sugar machinery factory of Mirrlees Watson in Tradeston, where there was a very well-organised Amalgamated Society of Engineers (ASE) branch. How far conditions were then from any later images of Red Clydeside is shown by McShane's fascinating account of this workplace in his book *No Mean Fighter*:

> There was a Tory shop steward there called Young, a likeable old
> fellow with a beard (which was rare then). He saw to it that
> everyone was a member of the ASE, but he was well in with the
> management. The foremen were also members of the ASE; the ASE

was a sort of religion to them... The members really believed themselves to be the aristocrats of labour and they dressed differently and better than other workers. Like all craftsmen they wore blue suits and bowler hats on week-ends, but during the week they wore a deep sea cap. They all thought they were marine engineers!

McShane also described the fascinating tradition of tossing the brick at Mirrlees:

> By tradition it was the engineers who 'tossed the brick' at the end of the Fair Holiday... after the ten-day holiday two or three hundred workers would meet outside the factory gate. One of them, one of the best known, often a freemason, would toss a brick in the air. If the brick didn't come down, we would start work, but if it did we would take another day's holiday... It wasn't a one-day strike, we just weren't very keen on working. Tossing the brick was a common practice in the engineering shops until the war broke out.

You have to ask, what odds were there against the brick *not* coming down?

Another neighbouring works to Howden's was the Clutha factory of Maclellan's, crane makers and structural engineers, in adjacent Kinning Park. They built the beautiful semi-circular glass and steel canopy at Glasgow's Queen Street Station, which still stands today, though the fine frontage to George Square was blocked out by redevelopment. Both works were still in operation until the 1980s when they finally closed, but Howden's operates in a smaller plant a couple of miles west of here at Craigton. One of the last things Howden's built at Scotland Street were the boring machines for the Channel Tunnel.

On leaving the Howden's works, it is interesting to take a walk north up Carnoustie Street, under the motorway, and through the deadlands around it, to the former Co-operative building – or complex of buildings – in Morrison Street. Although 1906 saw the official birth of the Labour Party, and in areas such as Kingston and Kinning Park many of the skilled workers were organised in trades unions, it was the Co-operative that at this time was by far the most important organisation in working-class life. The Scottish Co-operative Society was determined to show this with its headquarters and associated warehouses. While many of its members might have questioned the vast expense the buildings here entailed, they certainly showed that the Co-op was a rising power in the land. The buildings are municipal in size; indeed, the architects were accused of using their failed entry from Glasgow Municipal Chambers from 10 years earlier for the Co-op building, completed in 1897.

The 20th century saw the virtual collapse of the original ideals and aims of the co-operative movement, and the present buildings have been converted to luxury flats and offices. A block away is the building that till recently was the Co-op Funeral Directors' premises. I was once examining the sculpted reliefs on this building, when the unavoidable Glasgow punter appeared, to watch what I was doing. 'Aye, son,' he said, 'the Co-op isnae whit it wis. But it will still bury ye.' Going east along Paisley Road, the gradual repopulation of Kingston illustrated by the Co-op flats is emphasised by a more modest set of houses, the Riverview development, built on the infilled Kingston Dock in the 1980s, to the north of the Co-op.

Paisley Road becomes Kingston Street, and one is now actually in Tradeston, where most of the housing was either demolished or decapitated, leaving only the ground-floor shops and pubs remaining. Almost alone of traditional housing remaining here is the fine former fire station on Wallace Street, with its firemen's houses, which are reached down Centre Street from Kingston Street. These dwellings were converted into offices before the idea of repopulating the inner cities became fashionable. But in Tradeston, too, there is growing repopulation: now-disused warehouses, of which there are many striking examples, as well as factories, are being restored as apartments. However welcome these developments are, we still seem to be, literally, building ourselves problems for the future. Conspicuously absent in all these developments are any family housing units, and even more so, any social, rented housing. The poor are being built out of inner-city redevelopment, and one wonders if a population of sinkies, dinkies and skiers is a viable social basis for any community.[1]

Passing back along Wallace Street and then under the Kingston Bridge, one re-enters Kingston proper. Here was formerly the main mineral terminal for Glasgow and the west of Scotland, where iron ore and coal

---

[1] Sinkies, single income, no kids; dinkies, double income, no kids; skiers, spending the kids' inheritance, i.e. affluent retirees.

as well as other materials were unloaded by huge cranes, and then taken by rail to their destinations. Disused by the early 1980s, these cranes were blown up and the area redeveloped. Unfortunately, this redevelopment took place at a time when Glasgow was desperate for anything that would be income-bearing, and the area here is an eyesore of the kind one sees in cities in the United States. Cinemas, bingo halls and similar constructions of little architectural merit blot the Springfield Quay area of the riverside – Uglification in its classic form.

On the positive side, a little further downriver at Mavisbank Gardens lies an exciting, mixed development of housing in a variety of shapes and colours, which gives a vibrancy to the riverside, contrasting with the tack of Springfield Quay. But again, this is a middle-class ghetto, separated from the community around Paisley Road to the south. And here on Paisley Road, for the first time in our walk, we come into real urban bustle, as demolition in this area was not as enthusiastic as elsewhere around.

Many of the finest buildings in areas like this were built by the progressive Glasgow City Council of the time. The schools, the fire stations and others still stand where their neighbours have fallen. A good example is given here on Paisley Road with the Kingston Halls and Library, built in 1904, again, a brand-new building when Scotland Street School enrolled its first pupils. The halls and library have long since closed and the building today is used as a lodging house, whose inhabitants add a touch of local colour to the proceedings of the street.

As we head towards Paisley Road Toll, the street fills with buildings and their associated inhabitants. Until 1905, here on Paisley Road (known affectionately to locals as 'the PR'), within a couple of hundred yards you could enter three independent burghs. Just west of Kingston Docks you left Glasgow Corporation behind, and a stone's throw past the Paisley Toll, you entered the independent burgh of Govan. Between lay the smallest, most densely populated – and one of the shortest lived – burghs in Scottish history, Kinning Park. At its narrowest, northern apex, Kinning Park was less than 200 yards across. Originally part of Govan, the locals had seceded in 1871 and established their Lilliputian burgh of 100 acres and 6,000 people. By 1882, it had its own town hall, police force, fire service, public baths and schools. By the time of its annexation by Glasgow in 1905, Kinning Park had a population of

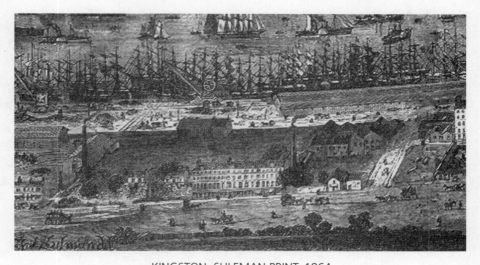

KINGSTON, SULEMAN PRINT, 1864
The docks were in full operation 20 years later.
Note the continued predominance of sailing ships, even in the 1860s

14,000. And since half the burgh was industry and public buildings, the population density was truly staggering. Even today, it is the most populated area between the Gorbals and Govan.

Kinning Park 'Cross' would have been where the Angel Building now stands, named after its crowning sculpture, the gilded angel atop its roof pavilion. Often called the 'Govan Angel', the building was actually in Kinning Park burgh when it was erected in 1890. A high-quality construction, it, and the associated tenements around, has survived redevelopment to provide a pleasing coherence to this pocket of Glasgow. The ground floor was once a gents' outfitters, Ogg Brothers, still fondly remembered locally, and is now an Italian restaurant, La Fiorentina. Surprisingly, situated in a spot like this, it is an excellent, award-winning eatery, and a useful place for refreshment on your perambulations. As an alternative, across the road is the Old Toll Bar, reasonable enough on the exterior, but inside possibly Glasgow's finest 19th-century pub, with fine-cut glass and mahogany interior. One reason the exterior of the Old Toll Bar is less impressive is that its Victorian windows were smashed in a riot during the Glasgow rent strike of 1915.

On the north side of the road stands the Grand Old Opry. Many will know that the original of this venue lies in Nashville, Tennessee, but for three nights each week, Nashville comes to the Paisley Road as busloads of cowboys and cowgals from Glasgow, and from Wild West towns such as Larkhall and Blantyre, arrive at the Opry to listen to country music, line dance, eat beans at the chuck wagon, and engage in simulated shoot-outs at the PR corral. Not a place for the faint-hearted around 11 p.m., but a wonderful example of the inordinate capacity that the Glasgow working class have of enjoying themselves.

Once I was with some friends in the Old Toll Bar before going across the road to the Opry. The bartender, seeing we were not regulars, gave us some sage advice: 'Oh, aye, yiz'll be welcome there. But jist a wee wurd o' advice. Dinnae laugh at the shoot-oots, or yooze could be back in here quicker than ye think.'

The Kinning Park/Govan boundary generally followed Paisley Road West from here; Govan to the north, Kinning Park to the south. But a small loop included a couple of tenement blocks on the north side, behind the Angel, in the pocket burgh. Here lay Rutland Crescent, which used to have a primary school where the great Clydeside socialist agitator John Maclean taught, before being dismissed from his post at another school in 1914 for his opposition to the war. Both he and his sidekick, James MacDougall, were very active in the Labour movement in this part of Glasgow, standing for both municipal and parliamentary elections. Though never elected, they polled respectable numbers of votes, running into thousands. 'Doon the PR' there are new houses, lining the street as houses should, and several of these are low-cost private housing or rented social housing developments, which is welcome to see.

Going down Admiral Street to Kinning Park south of the PR gives us an idea of what the district must have been like before redevelopment and road building – but it requires some imagination. Under the motorway lie many streets that connected this area to the industrial districts in the south of the burgh, around McLellan Street. This latter, now a road on a trading estate, was once reputed to be the longest street of tenements in Glasgow; today, not one tenement remains. Under the M8 motorway itself lies the original ground of Rangers Football Club before it moved to Ibrox, as well as the site of the former Burgh Hall, which was at the bottom of Stanley Street, now abruptly truncated. Rangers won nothing while they were here from 1876 to 1887, though Queens Park did. At a Scottish Cup Final at Kinning Park in 1881, they beat Dumbarton by

GLASGOW WORKMAN, JOSEPH HERMAN, 1940
A fine and sympathetic study of the kind of unskilled labourer who would have found
work at the docks

two goals to one. You would take your life in your hands trying to 'kick a baa' on the former ground now! Plantation Park, at Cornwall Street is small, since over half of it went to the motorway, and Cornwall Street continues on the far side of the motorway. Atlantis sank beneath the waves; much of Kinning Park, and Kingston, sank beneath the M8.

Surprisingly, much remains of fascination to the curious in the residues of Scotland's mini burgh, walking along Milnpark Street and its side roads. Apart from engineering, the main industry here was food production, and the principal factory, operating from 1860 to 1990, was Grey Dunn's biscuit works in Stanley Street, now part empty and part used for storage. One of the Grey family was the last Provost of Kinning Park. In the same street is a huge complex of a derelict school and ancillary buildings, the former Catholic church of Our Lady and St Margaret's with the associated seminary. This reminds us that the weans here would have seen from the school windows the place where many of them would spend their working lives – in the biscuit factory just across the road – just as the Scotland Street pupils would have done with Howden's. The school is being restored as Glasgow social work department offices. Harry McShane attended this school in the 1890s to receive what he called a 'minimal education', consisting in large part of religious instruction. He noted that it was then a brutal place. The headmaster would cane pupils and make them run around the school with their trousers at their heels, while 'the priests only came in to hit some child for not being at Mass'.

Not all industry in Kinning Park has closed down. Indeed, on part of the site of the former Maclellan's Clutha works, across the M8, is one of Glasgow's industrial success stories of recent years, the factory of the Asian-owned Trespass clothing company. But with 200 workers, it employs only a fraction of what Maclellan's did. Also, in the handsome former Kingston Engine Works on the corner of Milnpark Street and Portman Street, the multi-national media empire of News International opened its Scottish works in the late 1980s, after breaking the print unions in the strike at Wapping in 1987. If only that strike had succeeded, and Murdoch had become bankrupt, we might have been spared some of the worst excesses of the degeneracy of the media over the past two decades.

In the former Kinning Park Bakery on the corner of Stanley Street and Milnpark Street, Rupert Murdoch's News International had a neighbour of a very different political complexion. Here was situated the headquarters of the Scottish Socialist Party (SSP), with its walls festooned by examples of agitprop folk art. Appropriately, since he was very active in this part of Glasgow, there is a mural commemorating John Maclean. On a visit a couple of years ago, I suggested to one of their activists, smoking outside the building, that the murals must have been done a while back, since they showed Tommy Sheridan with a full head of hair. Tommy's troubles have doubtless caused him to lose even more hair as the promising start made by the SSP has degenerated into infighting, and has led, at the time of writing, to their headquarters being put on the market to pay the party's debts. I hope the murals at least will remain.

The SSP was a positive addition to the political scene in Scotland initially, managing to organise amongst the marginalised sections of the working class, who were ignored by other parties, and waging effective campaigns against the poll tax and water privatisation. Once the SSP gained Holyrood representation they became the court jesters of the establishment, media celebrities noted more for their personal lives than any political effectiveness, and set up for a fall which inevitably came. But without them, who will speak for the voiceless? As Brecht said in *Threepenny Opera*:

> Some are in darkness
> And some are in light
> We see those in the light
> Those in darkness we don't.

Portland Street joins Scotland Street West, which once was a continuous road of fine sandstone tenements on both sides, which would have taken you straight to Mackintosh's school. The remaining houses on the north side of the street give an example of what was lost. Kinning Park subway station is at the end of our journey. It stands, like a concrete pillbox of the Second World War, on a grassed-over area, where there were tenements until the 1970s. The Clockwork Orange (the local term for the Glasgow subway) will take you from here back to central Glasgow.

Redevelopment in the Kingston–Tradeston–Kinning Park area, of what was seen for many years as a no man's land for human habitation, will bring both its opportunities and its problems. Plans must be realistic, but at the same time, they must aim high. In the centre of town, Glasgow School of Art, Mackintosh's greatest masterpiece, is still in use as a functioning art school. Is it totally impossible to think that one day, with the repopulation of this area, his Scotland Street School could again function not as a museum – welcome though that option was as an alternative to neglect and demolition – but as an actual school? Could it once again be the jewel in the crown?

CHAPTER 9

Paisley:
The Poverty of Philanthropy

AS AN ABERDONIAN living in Glasgow, I can empathise with the inhabitants of Paisley, known as 'Buddies', who are often accused of meanness.
People who will 'pick your pocket for a penny' rather than being 'buddies
willing to spare a dime' is how Glaswegians or the burghers of neighbouring Renfrew see people from Paisley. But more than this empathy
born of a shared stigma draws me to Paisley often.

Of all the multitude of contiguous satellite towns round my adoptive
Glasgow, it is Paisley which I find the most interesting. It has a fascinating 1,000 years' history, almost as long as Glasgow's, and, for a town of
75,000 people, a very rich-built environment recalling that history. Paisley
has made repeated, failed attempts to gain city status – with towns of
lesser historical and architectural merit such as Stirling and Inverness
beating it to the finishing line. But I think the description 'Scotland's
largest town' fits better with the local character. Whether or not they are
mean, the Buddies are certainly a cocksure lot with a good conceit of themselves and their town, and not without reason. In fact, being regarded as
'Glasgow's most interesting satellite' would probably be regarded as an
insult to Paisley's perceived high status. An eminent, but misinformed,
visitor to the town in the 1870s was famously informed by an irate town
council that 'Paisley is *not* a suburb of Glasgow'. Remember that and you
will be welcome.

Buddies are also more reserved than Glaswegians, possibly a little sus-
picious of 'Ootlanders' – and have a deserved reputation for clannishness.
'May you die in Paisley' was an old blessing here. In Paisley, there is less
of the gallus street theatre and constant banter of Glasgow, where in 10
minutes you can become a man's best friend (or enemy). And here again,
in their reserve, Buddies remind me of my native Aberdonians. One possible explanation for this is that most of Paisley's population were
recruited from neighbouring Lanarkshire, Renfrewshire and Ayrshire.

From being a small Scottish town, Paisley became a very large Scottish town. In 1900 only five per cent of Paisley's population was Irish born, and one per cent Highland born, compared with five times that number of each grouping in neighbouring Glasgow.

If they carried over the small town Scottish reserve to Scotland's biggest town, why are Paisley folk called 'Buddies'? The word has nothing to do with the familiar Americanism, meaning close friend. The term was in use by the early 19th century when writers spoke of Paisley 'bodies', the old Scottish word here simply meaning people or folk. Pronounced as 'buddies' (as in 'gin a body meet a body' in Burns's 'Comin thro' the Rye'), the term has struck, and is now spelt as it sounds.

A short quarter-of-an-hour train journey from Glasgow Central brings you to Paisley Gilmour Street Station, a fine mock-Tudor castellated building, with the platforms on a raised viaduct. If you look carefully around at platform level, behind the grime you will see much of the 19th century wood and ironwork still intact, only awaiting a lick of paint to make it stunning. Why do we not treat our cathedrals of transport as they deserve? The Gothic-revival post office of 1892, just outside the station on County Square, has fared better, being converted to a pub and restaurant, and its red sandstone exterior is still in fine condition. On the south side of the square, a late 18th century terrace needs only some cosmetic work to be a delightful cameo. Nothing short of demolition, however, could improve the ghastly shopping centre making up the fourth side of the square, a site which was occupied by the town's 19th century jail and courthouse until 1971.

Paisley itself has no cathedral, but on emerging from the station and going down Gilmour Street to the Cross, the eye is inevitably caught, across the waters of the White Cart, by the 800-year-old Paisley Abbey, a visual delight in both exterior and interior. A church has been here since the Celtic monastery associated with St Mirin, and later a priory, and then the abbey was founded in the 13th century. The Norman foundation was partly destroyed by the English in the wars of independence and in 1553 the tower collapsed. Though continuing as Paisley Parish Church, the present abbey is, to a great extent, a late 19th and 20th century reconstruction by eminent architects including Anderson and Robert Lorimer.

The west door is the main Norman relic, and the nave the main medieval one, and inside is the eighth century Barochan Cross, and a frieze of carved panels illustrating the life of St Mirin. The abbey hosts frequent concerts by the excellent Abbey Choir. The adjacent Place (i.e. palace) of Paisley survived the Reformation and was a mansion-house and then a slum dwelling, and for a while a public house, before restoration. During this restoration, streets of densely packed slums, which had blocked out the Abbey, were demolished to create the open vista of today.

Though founded as an ecclesiastical centre, it was the development of the textile industry in the 18th century and even further in the 19th century that made Paisley world famous and for a while Scotland's third largest centre of population after Glasgow and Edinburgh. Just south of the Abbey at the Hammill's waterfall on the Cart stands the imposing bulk of one of Paisley's former mills, now sympathetically converted into flats. This was the Anchor Mill, which was founded in 1812 by the Clark family to harness the power of the Cart, and the mill underwent continuing expansion for almost a century. Here was first produced thread wound on wooden spools, of the kind which I can still remember from my childhood days. These spools, or bobbins, were recyclable, and when returned to the haberdasher's awarded a half-penny off the price of a new reel of cotton thread.

Visible from the Anchor Mill is the huge lum of the Abbey Mill, also built by the Clarks, which is now a business centre. Walking from the Anchor Mill to the Abbey Mill gives you an idea of the size of this industrial undertaking, which in 1900 was one of the biggest textile factories in the world, with over 4,000 workers. Both mills still stand, and in the space between, which was occupied by the Clarks' factories various ancillary buildings, a supermarket and a couple of housing estates have been built with room to spare. Along with the Coats family, who established a similar huge thread works at Ferguslie in Paisley, the Clarks dominated industrial and social life in Paisley throughout the 19th century.

By 1870, Paisley was described as 'the dirtiest and most unhealthy town in Scotland' and rather more favourably, another observer had commented: 'The town was full of smoky grime and industrial vigour, drunken squalour and puritanical religion.' It was one of the fastest growing towns in the whole of the UK, prompting the Tory Prime Minister Disraeli to comment 'Keep your eye on Paisley'. But it was poor. In the 1820s, handloom weavers could earn over £1 a week, but the weekly wage for a female in the thread mills in the 1870s was less than half of that.

MILL LASSIES, c.1900
Many with shawls – and a few with fine bonnets

Just west of the Abbey is the Clark Town Hall, which must be one of the most imposing examples of such a structure in any town in Scotland. Fitting indeed, because continually failing in its efforts to become a city, Paisley is still Scotland's largest town. The burgh's population peaked around 1970 at 90,000, but like other industrial towns in recent decades it has lost population, and now has 75,000 inhabitants. The town hall was built in 1882, helped by £20,000 of funds provided by the Clark family, whose name graces the building, and the statue of George Clark, by the firm of Mossman, stands outside. Further marble busts of members of the Clark family are found at the entrance to the town hall. These entrepreneurs were not just after money, but immortality. And in the days before death duty and inheritance tax, such sums were petty cash. The Clarks' bequest to the town hall was less than three per cent of the fortune John Clark left in his will in 1894.

Still in use for social functions, the Clark Town Hall's role has been transferred to the quite ghastly Renfrewshire Council offices to the east of the Abbey. Around the area of the town hall and the Cross are what must stand as the largest collection of public sculptures in Scotland outside of Glasgow and Edinburgh city centres. As well as those of the Clarks mentioned are the statues of luminaries of the Coats dynasty by Rhind at the northern end of Dunn Square, as well as the obligatory statue of Queen Victoria in the square itself. An excellent short leaflet is available on these, and the other public sculptures of Paisley, from the tourist information office in Gilmour Street.

But the Buddies have not neglected recognition for their town's less affluent citizens. In Abbey Close, Paisley's greatest weaver-poet Robert Tannahill is commemorated in this open-air sculpture park, as is the less well known Alexander Wilson. Less well known in Scotland that is, than in the United States, where the self-educated weaver emigrated and became regarded as the founder of North American ornithology. A memorial frieze commemorates Wilson's childhood playground at the Hammills.

Tannahill's fate was less happy. He killed himself when his poetry failed to extricate him for the drudgery of the loom. The melancholy cast of his mind is evident in many of his poems:

Keen blaws the wind o'er the braes o' Gleniffer
The auld castle's turrets are covered wi' snaw
How changed fae the time when I met wi' my lover
Amang the brume bushes by Stanely green shaw.

His cottage lies a little to the west of the town centre, on Queen Street, a place of pilgrimage for his devotees, as well as the meeting place of the Paisley Burns Club, which Tannahill founded in 1805. Formerly 'thackit', the cottage is now slated. Tannahill's best known poem is probably 'Wild Mountain Thyme'.

Before the coming of factory methods of production, Paisley was a centre of hand-loom weaving. Versatile, the 'wabsters' could turn their hand to linen, silk or cotton. Their fame was recorded by Burns, when he dressed the graveyard temptress in Tam o' Shanter in 'Her cutty sark, o' Paisley harn'. Like many of their brethren, the Paisley weavers were radicals in politics and religion, but to an even greater extent were given to composing poetry. Radicalism and Paisley went together: possibly because Paisley remained, until comparatively recently, one of the poorest towns in Scotland. (Poverty may also be the source of the Buddies' alleged meanness.) As one local rhymster put it:

Paisley's name is widely spread
And history doth show it's
Been famed alike for shawls and thread,
For poverty and poets.

The Paisley weavers were a radical lot, given to strikes and rioting in
defence of their wages long before the ideas of the ideas of French
Revolution came along. The weavers, educated and intelligent, adopted
those ideas to a man. As Alexander Wilson put it:

The Rights of man are noo well kenned
And read by many a hunder
And Tammy Paine the buik has penned
And lent the Court a lounder.[1]

Wilson escaped to America when powerful local dignitaries were
offended by his writings, and also escaped from the loom, which he did
not love. One book of his poems was called *Groans from the Loom*.

In 1819, there was a week's rioting in Paisley High Street as the
authorities tried to suppress demonstrations in favour of parliamentary
reform, and in the Radical War of 1820 nowhere was more radical than
Paisley, when thousands of local workers went on strike and some went
as far as to take up arms for political reform. In a series of treason trials in
that year in the town, the defendants were acquitted. Paisley's radicalism
continued into the Chartist period in the 1830s and 1840s, when a surprising local leader of the agitation to gain working men the vote was
the Church of Scotland minister, Reverend Patrick Brewster. His denunciations of the rich and powerful at a time when poverty was endemic
and cholera rampant meant that he was passed over for the post of main
minister at the Abbey when it became vacant.

The weaving part of Paisley's industrial history is commemorated in
the Sma' Shot Cottages in Shuttle Street, just a short walk from the
Town Hall, which show how the weavers lived and worked. The most
scenic route is along Forbes Place, by the side of the Cart, and then by
Causeyside Street and New Street. At the entry to New Street, it is worth
stopping to admire the Russell Institute, another charitable endowment

---

[1] *Lounder*: severe blow.

'to buddies from a buddy' – the donor being one Mrs Russell. Built in 1923 as a child clinic by a local architect named James Maitland, it is probably Paisley's greatest 20th century building. Dawson's sculptures of mothers and children complement this beaux art masterpiece. Today, it is a family planning centre.

No such social welfare was available for the weavers in the Sma' Shot Cottages, whose lives can be re-lived on Wednesday and Saturday afternoons in the summer months. In their restored form these are very picturesque buildings, but the life of the weaver became harder and harder as the 19th century progressed. Faced with competition from factory production and power-driven Jaquard looms from the 1830s, the hand-loom weaver worked longer and longer hours for less and less pay. In 1832, Cobbet said 'the weavers of Paisley are covered in rags and half-starved'. There were 7,000 weavers in the 1830s, but by 1900, less than 100 hand-loom weavers remained.

Just close by the Sma' Shot Cottages lies Paisley Arts Centre in a con-verted church, the old Laigh (or low) Kirk, which was Paisley's second kirk after the Abbey itself. This was the Paisley charge of John Witherspoon before he emigrated to America and became the principal of Princeton Presbyterian College in 1768. Witherspoon is more famous as being the only clergyman to sign the US Declaration of Independence in 1776. Though he was not a Buddy by birth, Paisley is milking Witherspoon for all his worth, and a huge statue of the theologian has been erected recently outside Paisley University, which has established links with Princeton University through the Witherspoon connection.

Witherspoon Street takes you to Storie Street and then a left turn along Wellmeadow Street lands you in front of the imposing bronze-cast monument to Paisley's adoptive son. Executed by Alexander Stoddart, Paisley cunningly gifted a copy of the sculpture to Princeton. Who says Buddies are mean? Interestingly, Witherspoon left Paisley after his attempts to reform the morals of the population had largely failed, and even landed him in court on a libel charge.

Stoddart is also in the process of executing a sculpture of Paisley's prodigal son, Willie Gallacher, legendary figure of the Red Clydeside era and Communist MP for West Fife. Gallacher was born in Paisley, and his childhood is described in the early part of his book, *Revolt on the Clyde*. But he spent most of his life in political struggles in Glasgow, where he was a prominent figure in the Clyde Workers' Committee and the strikes during the First World War. Thereafter, his work amongst the Fife miners resulted in him becoming their MP in 1935. Though spending most of his active life away from Paisley, Gallacher returned to the town, and died in a council flat in 1965. Forty-thousand people followed his coffin, draped in the red flag, to Woodside Crematorium and a further 60,000 lined the streets. Stoddart has also been commissioned to commemorate another local Buddy, architect Thomas Tait, and one of Britain's foremost in the 20th century. He was responsible for St Andrew's House in Edinburgh and Tait's Tower at the Glasgow 1938 Empire Exhibition.

But to return to our promenade. On the opposite side of Wellmeadow Street from Witherspoon's statue we can see more examples of Paisley philanthropy, rather than Paisley parsimony. The Museum and Art Gallery, funded by contributions from the town's wealthy textile capitalists, especially the Coats, lies across from the university, as does the Thomas Coats Memorial Church of 1894, paid for by the family and notable more for its vast bulk – the size of many a cathedral – rather than any great architectural quality, in my opinion. But it made sure that the Buddies would never forget the Coats. Surprisingly for Presbyterian Paisley, Thomas Coats was a Baptist, and as a result this is a Baptist church.

Thomas Coats died in 1883, and was followed by his great rival John Clark in 1894. Competition between the firms gave way to price fixing as time progressed, and then came amalgamation, when Coats swallowed up the Clarks' concern in 1896. Further expansion and acquisitions followed, and by 1913 Coats was Britain's largest textile company, capitalised at almost £8 million, and employing 40,000 workers worldwide – only 12,000 of these in Scotland. Indeed, it was one of the first multi-nationals, operating in Russia, the United States and Spain.

In 1910, Coats' profits were £3.2 million, bigger than the profits of the second (Imperial Tobacco) and third (Guinness brewers) most profitable British industrial companies combined. The Coats had a mansion in Ferguslie, an estate at Glentanar on Deeside, and a collection of yachts, one which was 500 feet in length and steam driven. To their lucky 40,000 shareholders they were paying a staggering 25 per cent annual dividend in the early 20th century. But what about the workers? Those 40,000 were not so lucky; those in Paisley, for example, mostly living on less than £1 a week.

The Coats, like the Clarks, were paternalistic employers. As well as giving generously to charity, they also supported sickness and pension schemes for their workers. But they paid low wages, and with a largely female and non-unionised labour force, were able to get away with this for almost the first century of their existence as a firm. In the early years of the 20th century, this paternalistic consensus began to break down. In 1904, 1,000 boys at the mill went on strike, and the following year 3,000 of the mill girls followed suit. These were disorganised actions, with little effect. But many had been alerted to the plight of the mill workers, and several prominent outsiders, such as Keir Hardie the Independent Labour Party MP, and trades union organisers were active, earning the fierce denunciations of the Coats family, including Thomas Glen Coats, who was Paisley's Liberal MP at that time.

In 1907, the bulk of the workers at the Anchor Mill, 4,000-strong, came out and decided to march to the Ferguslie Mill and bring out their fellows. There followed a blockade of Ferguslie, with the police defending it from the strikers and preventing their entry. The police, with difficulty, retained control, and one reason for their problems was the novel method the mill lassies had of close combat. Realising their physical weakness against burly policemen, they would remove their hat pins and contact some delicate party of a policeman's anatomy. Coats cleverly gave the entire Ferguslie workforce time off on full pay during the strike, to prevent them joining it. Eventually the isolated Anchor workers went back to work, having won some concessions.

The pattern spread to other mills of the Coats empire, including their thread factory at Neilston, where the workers came out on strike in May 1910. The *Paisley Daily Express* described the scene:

On Wednesday evening a force of about 30 police was unable to cope with the crowd, fully 5,000 strong. The manager has been a marked man and his house the target for many missiles. The windows of the mills are all more or less shattered.

With support from other workers, the mill girls organised a 2,000-strong 'march of indignation' to the general manager's house in Pollokshields. This event was described by one of the organisers:

MILL LASSIES ON STRIKE, 1907
Mêlée caused by the girls sticking bonnet pins in the policemen

It can be easily understood that to lead such a disorderly, undisciplined horde of young girls, to whom the whole thing was more of a joke than anything else [they were carrying effigies of the manager which were intended to be burned] was by no means an easy job... The march, with a great banging of tin cans and shouting and singing, made its noisy way to Pollokshields where the respectable inhabitants were thoroughly disturbed.

A century of paternalism and workers' loyalty to their Liberal employers was coming to an end. After the First World War, no textile capitalist would ever again be elected in Paisley as the local MP.

Marx wrote an early work called *The Poverty of Philosophy*. He felt that philosophy had nothing to offer in resolving society's problems, indeed he had earlier famously stated that 'the philosophers have only interpreted the world, the point remains, to change it'. *The Poverty of Philanthropy* could sum up the history of Paisley. In 1900, Paisley had undoubtedly benefited more from charitable benefactions than any comparable town; yet it remained probably the poorest place in Scotland, with almost 50 per cent of the population living in officially overcrowded accommodation and infant mortality rates of 100 per 1,000 – twice the Scottish average. Dominated by textiles and female labour, it remained a low-wage economy. People imagine textiles as a 19th century industry, but Paisley's reign as thread capital of the world lasted much longer. Indeed, in 1950, the Anchor and Ferguslie works employed more than 10,000 people between them, more than they had ever employed in the Victorian era, and even in the 1960s there were still 5,000 at Coats Paton, as it was by then called. This was not much less than working at the new giant Rootes car plant at Linwood on Paisley's outskirts, by then the main local employer. But in less than a generation, both old and new industries have vanished.

Paisley has weathered the virtual collapse of the Scottish manufacturing industry better than many towns in the west of Scotland. One sign of this is that Paisley is the only location outside Scotland's cities which continues to produce a daily newspaper, the *Paisley Daily Express*, which has appeared since 1874 and still sells over 10,000 copies a day. Paisley University, now the West of Scotland University, created in 1992 from an amalgamation of various institutes of higher education, helps, as does the proximity of the region's biggest private employer, Glasgow Airport, many of whose 15,000 workforce come from Paisley.

But as we go west from the university, Wellmeadow Street bears unmistakeable scenes of urban decay – though the main area of urban deprivation in the town, Ferguslie Park, with 45 per cent of the population economically inactive, lies outside the town centre. A sharp turn up West Brae appears initially to give us more of the same, in a series of semi-derelict cottage buildings, but in the space of a hundred yards we are in a different world – the world of Oakshaw, one of the most delightful and interesting streetscapes in Scotland, and with one of the best views.

Ascending West Brae, a large cupola'd building is evident. Though known irreverently by the Buddies as the 'Parritch Pot' due to its inverted shape, this is Paisley's 19th century architectural masterpiece, built between 1849 and 1852 by Charles Wilson, who was the architect of much of Glasgow's prestige Park Circus area. Again it is a product of Paisley philanthropy, the John Neilson Institution being built as a school after a £22,000 bequest by a local grocer of that name. It was meant for children of the poor and orphans, and provided food and clothing as well as education. Some in Glasgow felt Paisley was getting above itself,

ASQUITH, LIBERAL MP FOR PAISLEY,
1920–24

The last in almost a century of Liberal
MPs for Paisley

hiring such an eminent architect to build the institution, and 'erecting a palace where a poorhouse would have been more to the purpose' (Hugh MacDonald, *Rambles Round Glasgow*, 1854).

Now flats, the Institution building is not accessible, but a walk round it to the belvedere at Oakshawhead gives a fine view of the building and on a clear day the view extends north to the Campsies and Ben Lomond. Although it is true that many of Paisley's finest buildings date from after the writing of MacDonald's book, it is surprising to find him, who visited Oakshaw, commenting: 'In general architectural appearance the town of Paisley presents few features calling for the particular attention of the tourist.' 'That's Glasgow for ye', the Buddies would say.

Oakshaw Street is an eclectic mix of architectural styles and periods. There is housing of recent construction alongside 18th century religious buildings, such as the Old Manse, and the Gaelic Chapel of 1793. There are staid 19th century tenements beside flamboyant revivalist buildings of the same century, such as the Brough Nursing Home, and on each side of the street enticing cobbled lanes lead downwards to hidden corners calling for exploration. There is the Paisley Philosophical Institution rooms (and Camera Club) and the splendidly spired Oakshaw Trinity Church, one of the last of the many kirks still in use here.

And, as ever, there are examples of Paisley benevolence, of charity beginning at home. The Hutcheson Charity School flourished in the 19th century until the pupils were transferred to the more palatial premises of the John Neilson. And, of all things, the street hosts an observatory, the Coats Observatory, gifted by Thomas Coats in 1883 but now run by

Paisley Museums – and still functioning. This is one of the first
wheelchair-friendly (with ramp
access) buildings ever constructed,
as Thomas Coats, who was astro-
nomically minded, was himself con-
fined to a wheelchair later in life.

Dropping down Oakshaw
Street east to School Wynd brings
you back to County Square and the
rail station. If time permits and the
body demands sustenance, a walk
along High Street and down New
Street to the Bull Inn will land you
in a pub which claims – with some
justification – to be the best Art
Nouveau hostelry in the country,
though I can think of a couple of
rivals in Glasgow. This will also
allow a study of the fine – if some-

WILLIE GALLACHER
'Buddy' and Communist MP for the Fife
miners. His funeral attracted almost
100,000 people

what faded – glories of some of the buildings in the High Street, such as
the YMCA building and the Liberal Club. Built in 1886, the latter
expressed the domination of 19th century Paisley by Liberalism, in the
way that the 20th century was to become dominated by Labourism –
Paisley electing its first Labour MP in 1924. The Labour movement has,
however, left fewer memorials than its predecessor, apart from the fine Co-
operative building in Causeyside Street, and Willie Gallacher's statue –
when it is finally built.

I am unsure whether I have acquitted the Buddies of meanness, but
I hope I have convicted their town of fascination. Its name is mainly
known worldwide from the Paisley Pattern, the teardrop design made
famous by the Paisley Shawl. But the shawl era was a fairly short one in
the town's history, largely over by the 1870s, and that industry never
dominated the town in the way that thread-making did. Although you can
see the world's largest collection of shawls in the local museum, the pattern
of Paisley embraces much more than that famous design.

CHAPTER 10

Port Glasgow
Resurrection?

IN 2007, 300 YEARS after the Union of 1707, thoughts turned to a consideration of what political fusion with England had brought to Scotland. One thing it brought was Port Glasgow. The Union opened the markets of the American colonies to Glasgow's merchants, and they needed a port capable of berthing ships able to cross the Atlantic, which the then shallowness of the Clyde prevented the city itself providing. After the rather surprising and short-sighted refusal of the burghers of Dumbarton to undertake the role, Glasgow's merchants constructed a new harbour on the southern shore of the Clyde, moved the city's Custom House there in 1710, and the development soon took the name of Port Glasgow.

There was really nothing here beforehand besides Newark Castle, seat of the Maxwells. As an observer noted in 1655: 'besides the laird's house, [only] some four or five houses'. For the century after 1710, the new town was to be Glasgow's – and Scotland's – main trading port. By the 1730s, 50 ships were sailing from Port Glasgow to the West Indies and the Americas, bringing in cargoes of sugar, tobacco and, most of all, timber. Twenty-thousand tonnes of logs were imported every year and floated in rafts in ponds on the Clyde until needed. Many of the wooden stakes that enclosed the ponds can still be seen along the shoreline at low tide, and are often mistaken for old mussel scalps. Even in Edwardian times, photographs show the local harbour crammed with floating logs.

The year 2007 was another anniversary – that of the abolition of the slave trade in the British Empire, and it would be bad faith not to reflect on the contribution that slavery made to the growing wealth of Port Glasgow in the century following 1707. It is true that there were no slave markets in Port Glasgow – nor in Glasgow or Greenock – as there were in Liverpool or Bristol, but the Clyde was implicated in slavery, though to a lesser degree than were those ports. Port Glasgow-registered ships did engage in the slave trade, and the American and Caribbean

THE *COMET*, ON AN EARLY VOYAGE
Port Glasgow was the birthplace of steam navigation

plantations where the sugar and tobacco were produced were based on slave labour, and many of these were actually owned by Scottish merchants. Plantation slavery was one of the preconditions for the establishment of industrial wage-slavery.

Gradually industry followed to Port Glasgow in the wake of trade. Sugar refining was established early, followed by shipbuilding when Thomas McGill opened a boatyard close to Newark Castle in 1790. The Gourock Ropework Company moved here in 1797 from its original site, and manufactured ropes, nets and canvas for almost two centuries. Then, in 1812, a world-shattering event took place in Port Glasgow, when John Wood's shipyard built the *Comet*, the first steam-driven paddle steamer capable of sea voyages. This was followed three years later by the *Thames*, which made the epochal 500-mile journey from the Clyde to London. Port Glasgow had given birth to steam navigation. At the cutting edge of technology, as far back as 1760 the town had constructed Britain's first dry dock for ship repair, and Port Glasgow also opened the country's first gasworks in 1803.

The town was growing and prospering. In 1775 it achieved burgh status, and in 1815 its council commissioned one of Scotland's leading architects, David Hamilton, to build the classical burgh hall. Further improvements to the harbour took place, though Port Glasgow was gradually losing its position as Scotland's leading import–export location to its rival and better-sited neighbour, Greenock. But as its trading role declined Port Glasgow's industrial capacity increased. Although industries such as rope- and sail-making and sugar refining continued, the town soon came to be dominated by one industry – shipbuilding. And as further developments and concentration took place, this industry was more and more dominated by one company, the firm of Lithgows, originally known as Russell's. By 1931, Port Glasgow had a population of 21,000 people. In the 1920s, Lithgow's employed 8,000 men, equivalent to almost 70 per cent of the male labour force of the town. Monopolising the local labour market allowed Lithgow's to keep a downward pressure on wages that shipbuilders elsewhere envied.

William Lithgow started working in Reid and Co's shipyard, which had built the famous 'Floating Kirk' used at Strontian during the Disruption of the 1840s. Lithgow set up his own business in 1874 at the Kingston yard, building large cargo-carrying sailing ships. (The last surviving example of this type of vessel is the Clyde-built, steel-hulled cargo sailing ship, the *Glenlee*, which has been restored and will be a centrepoint of Glasgow's new Riverside Museum. The *Glenlee* was built at Port Glasgow in the 1890s, but not by Lithgow's.) Unlike his competitors, Lithgow built standardised boats, and then sought orders, rather than simply waiting on customers. He died in 1907 with an amassed fortune of £2 million (multiply by about 150 for today's values), a huge return on his original investment of £1,000.

His son James took over the business and again built standardised vessels – tramp steamers – which especially benefited the firm in wartime when mass-produced merchant shipping was needed to replace constant losses. Lithgow's expanded, acquiring yards in Greenock and also the famous Fairfield yard in Govan, and its chairman emerged as the recognised spokesman for the industry. Indeed, Sir James Lithgow as he was then known, became Controller of Merchant Shipbuilding and Repair during the Second World War. The war restored shipbuilding prosperity to the Clyde, and the post-war construction years continued the good times. It is easy to be wise after the event about the decline of shipbuilding, but when James Lithgow died in 1952, Britain was still the world's greatest shipbuilding nation, and the Lithgow group itself was the largest private shipbuilding form in the world.

But before that had come the crash of 1929–31. Lithgow's closed its doors, and an astonishing 92 per cent of men in Port Glasgow were out of work, the highest number ever recorded anywhere in the UK. Port Glasgow was probably the most poverty-stricken place in Scotland in the 1930s. In addition to the record unemployment levels, it was also the most densely inhabited town, with 45 per cent of the population overcrowded – even by the modest standards of that time. There were specific reasons why this was so. Port Glasgow was tiny, crammed in between the 19th century railway and the 18th century harbour, amounting to little more than a square mile in area. There was simply no place to re-house the population; when unfit buildings were demolished and replaced by better ones, overcrowding actually increased in the remaining housing stock, as the displaced moved in to sub-let property.

Repeatedly, neighbouring Greenock attempted to amalgamate with Port Glasgow, a measure which would have provided the necessary building space, but the local town council, dominated before the Second World War by the Birkmyre family of Gourock Ropeworks, successfully resisted amalgamation fearing that it would lead to a rise in business rates. Though it was cloaked in local patriotic jargon, this attitude helped condemn generations of Port Glasgow's inhabitants to dreadful housing conditions. The Birkmyres prospered, establishing a near-monopoly in their trade by buying competing works in Dundee and also the New Lanark mills.

This activity brought the Birkmyre family enormous wealth. Broadfield, built by David Bryce, was their mansion 'above the shop' in Port Glasgow itself. To this was added the estate of Dalmunzie in Perthshire, where the Birkmyres demonstrated a new level of conspicuous consumption by the construction of a private railway for stalking guests, complete with miniature stations, each bigger than the 'single end' houses their workers lived in. The Lithgows, not to be outdone, commissioned Robert Lorimer to build their Edwardian mansion at Gleddoch in the hills near Port Glasgow, and acquired a hunting estate in Argyll. But there was more co-operation than competition between the families. Henry Birkmyre's daughter, Agnes, married William Lithgow. Lithgow's yards bought Birkmyre's ropes and sails, and Birkmyre invested in Lithgow-built ships.

Port Glasgow today

Port Glasgow rail station does not speak, as Paisley's or Greenock's does, of former days of glory. Nevertheless, it is quietly pleasing, if fairly run down, and retains elements of its old glass, wood and iron Victorian and Edwardian fittings. A renovation of the station would have a better impact on visitors; first impressions are important. Going down the brae into the town leads you to the Star Hotel, built in Edwardian times for commercial travellers and those visiting the shipyards. Alas, very few people come to Port Glasgow now, and the Star is a hotel no more, merely a pub. Heading down John Wood Street one is surrounded by the tenements of the Edwardian slum clearance era, when the bay area of Port Glasgow was (possibly) the most densely populated part of the UK. For those who like statistics, population density here was 500 people per acre, compared with a Scottish urban average of 90.

These Edwardian houses are not of especially high quality and neither are the surrounding houses, dating from the 1930s and 1950s, when Port Glasgow, along with Greenock, developed a brutalist style in council housing that is hardly matched elsewhere in Scotland. Tarmacadamed back courts were an especial favourite of planners hereabouts. Tight budgets were partly to blame; but so too were small-town councils who were unable to attract real talent to their employ. Port Glasgow – and later Inverclyde's – architects and planners appear to have been trained in the use of little more than a pencil and ruler. A turn right at the bottom of John Wood Street takes you past the early 1970s' blocks of medium-rise flats, which were seen as the solution to the housing question at that time.

Just beyond this, however, is a wonderful building which shows that our much maligned Victorian forebears could combine functionalism with decoration, even with beauty. This ornamented red-brick building was originally a sugar refinery in 1860 before being taken over by the Gourock Rope Company in the 1880s, and subsequently expanded. At its height, 1,000 workers, mainly women, toiled here. The Gourock Rope Company had a long history, making the sails for the *Comet* and the hawser for the *Queen Mary* in 1936, before it finally closed in 1975. The works lay idle for 20 years and a demolition order was granted on the factory, with the outlying buildings suffering that fate. Inertia rather than imagination possibly saved the main building, and it is currently being restored as luxury apartments by developers. They are hoping that, at the very edge of the town and 15 minutes from Glasgow Airport – and just another 10 minutes to the city centre itself – this project will make a handsome return on any investment.

Restored, the old ropeworks will make a fine eastern entrance to the town, as already does a much older building across the Glasgow Road. The sadly little-known Newark Castle is another asset of Port Glasgow that was almost lost through lack of interest and neglect, but, now restored by Historic Scotland, it is well worth a visit. It is surprising that the castle survived at all, surrounded as it was until recently by overtowering ship-yards; many similarly placed historic buildings were simply flattened. The oldest surviving part of the castle is a 15th century tower house, built by the Maxwells, lords of Newark (new-werk, i.e. new construction). To this tower, Patrick Maxwell added an impressive Renaissance mansion in the 1590s. Above the doorway is the date 1597, and an inscription, 'The blissingis of God be herein'.

The Maxwells were well connected, and James IV stayed in the tower house in 1495 on his way to attempt the pacification of the Western Isles, leaving Newark on his ship, the *Flower*. Patrick Maxwell, above mentioned, was a close friend of James IV, which prevented him suffering for his many misdeeds, such as murdering the laird and eldest son of Skelmorlie in 1584. He made peace with the youngest son, cowering for his life, by saying, 'Robin, come doon tae me, wha has dane ye sae gude a turn, as tae mak ye young laird and auld laird o Skelmorlie in ae day.' He was also a wife beater, abusing and imprisoning his wife Margaret for many of the 44 years of their marriage until she escaped, after many unheeded appeals to the privy council for protection. The last laird, another Patrick, died in 1694 and the castle and lands were subsequently sold, and gradually the grounds parcelled out for industrial development. The castle survived, though it was never again inhabited.

Perhaps the most interesting part of the castle is the dookit, which I had mistaken for a sort of lighthouse, guiding ships across the Clyde to the castle. Deborah, the custodian on my visit, assured me that it was always a dookit and had been originally part of the barmekin wall, now gone, surrounding the castle. As it was not busy, she opened the dookit for me, showing me the maze of pigeon lofts, and also the stone seat, complete with lavatory with underground outlet to the sea, for the man who had to attend to the doos. Newark deserves more than the mere 2,000 visitors it gets a year.

Next to Newark Castle is possibly an even more surprising survival from the past – a shipyard. Or, at least, a boatyard, as Ferguson's Marine, the last yard to survive on the entire Inverclyde waterfront, employs around 300 men and builds mainly smaller craft such as ferries. Ferguson's is in fact the last merchant shipbuilder on the Clyde. A boat was on the stocks on my last visit, but the yard has suffered recently from competition from other European Union yards especially those in Poland, which Ferguson's management and local Inverclyde politicians claim are receiving hidden subsidies from their governments. Ferguson's may yet go the way of Lamont's yard which stood on the other side of Newark Castle, and which was closed, demolished and the ground landscaped in the 1990s. Soon Newark Castle may again stand, as it did formerly, surrounded by parkland.

The stroll back to central Port Glasgow takes you through Coronation Park, a 1950s creation which shows as much inspiration in its design as do the houses of the period. Again, ruler and pencil appear to have served to create this unimaginative green space, on what is a stunning waterfront with views across the Clyde to the Highland hills. This whole area used to be the harbour of Port Glasgow, which was infilled after the Second World War, as it was by then so little used. This had the unfortunate effect of separating the centre of the town from the waterfront, an injury doubled when a dual carriageway was built between Coronation Park and the town. Crossing this carriageway takes you past a sad-looking oblong portakabin-style structure with the inscription 'Old Men's Club', and to the pride and glory of Port Glasgow, the town hall. This was made redundant when the town became part of Inverclyde in 1975, but has been turned to good use as a well-equipped and pleasant library. It would benefit, however, from some kind of heritage exhibition or mini-museum.

Further along Bay Street we come to an example of open-air heritage, in the form a full-size replica of the original *Comet* of 1812, built by the apprentices at Lithgow's shipyard 150 years later. It is highly visible and well protected from vandalism, but the exhibit lacks any information about the *Comet* and its historical significance. On the wall opposite, across the dual carriageway, is a plaque mentioning that the boat was built hereabouts, but again, no information nor explanation of its

NEWARK CASTLE, PORT GLASGOW
This building survived the growth of the shipbuilding industry all around, and now stands restored, whilst most of the yards have closed.

PORT GLASGOW SHOPPING CENTRE
Ruler and pencil 1970s architecture at its worst. New shopping complexes are being built on the site of the old Lithgow shipyard.

world-historic significance is given. In 1912 thousands of people lined the streets of Port Glasgow, and thousands more took part in a parade, with bands and banners, to commemorate the centenary of the launch of the *Comet*. Does the town have the resilience to repeat this event in 2012?

Just opposite the *Comet* is the 1960s town centre of Port Glasgow, a concrete oblong of hideous appearance. If you have ever seen a worse piece of urban architecture, write and tell me about it. I entered here looking for a place for refreshment and eventually found a cholesterol café, where a cheese pastie seemed the least dangerous item of consumption.

'The oven's broke and I'll hae tae microwave it. Is that awright? Some o' them dinnae like their cheese pasties microwaved,' I was told.

I agreed to the experiment, as there appeared little alternative, but after consuming the limp offering, I had to concur that those locals who eschewed the delicacy of microwaved cheese pastie had good taste.

A whole new Port Glasgow town centre is being constructed, on the site of the former Lithgow's Kingston yard. Lithgow's was still recruiting workers in the '70s and '80s with the oil tanker boom and later North Sea construction work, of which they grabbed a sizeable chunk. But in the early 1990s, the yard finally closed down for good, and was flattened. The demolition included even its giant 225-tonne Goliath crane, constructed by the firm of Arrol, which was such a visible symbol and icon from many points on both banks of the Clyde. This should have been maintained for posterity, as was the case with Glasgow's famous Finnieston crane. New motorways and shopping centres are being built in the hundreds of acres of derelict land here, and one can only hope that the result will be an addition to the landscape of the Clyde and not another commercial development without architectural merit – but allow us 'tae hae wir doots'.

Down here in Ardgowan Street, off the Greenock Road, where the yard lay, it was very difficult to re-imagine the layout of the former yards amidst the ground clearance and new infrastructural developments. I was lucky enough to find a retired shipyard worker, Hugh, walking his dog, and he was able to describe it all as if the scene was still there.

'Ardgowan Street here,' he said, 'was tenements till the 1970s. They wis flattened tae expand the yard that was building huge tankers at the time. We built them in haufs and then joined them thegether. Then when the Japanese and the Koreans started coming, and we were training them, we knew the yards were finished. It's the weans I fear for. There's nae work for them here, nae real work. Ye cannae jist serve at check-oots till yer pension.'

To the Kingston yard in 1940 came another visitor, 'a feart wee man', as one of the female workers described him. Another commented that 'at first we all thought he was a tramp who had sneaked in at the gate'. He was Stanley Spencer, whom many critics consider Britain's greatest 20th century artist, and he had come to Port Glasgow to record the working practices of the shipyard as a war artist. His visit was arranged due to the influence exercised by Sir James Lithgow, who wanted the production techniques in his yards recorded. Lithgow was reputedly to be disappointed in what Spencer produced. The artist worked on and off in Port Glasgow, at first staying at the Star Hotel, and then in digs with local people, from 1940 to 1946. Spencer was soon accepted by the workforce as he wandered about Kingston yard, doing his drawings hurriedly on sheets of toilet paper and often giving these away to the workers, who affectionately regarded him as their yard mascot. During this period he produced a series of works of art that are quite unique.

Portrayals of working men in art are very rare. Even previous war artists, such as Muirhead Bone who had drawn in the shipyards in the First World War, tended to concentrate on the ships being built and the machinery used in their construction, rather than the workers themselves. Spencer irritated his employers, the War Artists' Advisory Committee, in that he did not paint a single image of a ship in six years. All his paintings are of the workers in the yard at their labour. Spencer's critics also felt his images gave no overall impression of the process of ship production, from design to finished product, but instead endlessly reproduced collections of workers all doing more or less the same task.

This was because Spencer, a highly religious man who claimed repeated personal encounters with God, saw the shipyard workers as engaged in some kind of religious ceremony. He found the yards to be like a church, 'dark and cozy and full of mysterious places and happenings', and spoke of the workers as follows:

They are like the angels in Paradise Lost, who had to hurl great pieces of rock at Satan's invading army... I wish to make what happens in the [working] day to be experienced as a kind of

Garden of Eden... I was as disinclined to disturb [their work] as
I would be to disturb a religious service.

As a result, Spencer's paintings, powerful as is their impact, bear little
relation to the realities of working people's lives. Spencer had a limited
understanding of the material processes of work involved, and his paintings
are full of technical mistakes and misunderstandings. In *Burners*, there
is a self-portrait of the artist, looking very puzzled. More importantly,
Spencer makes work which was hard and dangerous appear homely and
pleasant. This is clearest in Spencer's depiction of the men's clothes. He
garbs them in the remembered clothes of the villagers of his Edwardian
youth in the village of Cookham in Berkshire. The workers wear brightly
coloured waistcoats, and bright and clean checked tweeds, with neat
turn-ups and clean cloth caps. One worker commented, 'It was quite
comical to us, because all these workers had filthy jobs. But he painted
their clothes as checks, glowing bright checks, red and yellow.'[1]

The impact of Port Glasgow on Spencer was profound. He felt he
had discovered a religiosity to the collective labour and collective social
life of the workers to such an extent that he thought the Resurrection
itself might take place in Port Glasgow. On a walk one evening past the
cemetery, he wrote, 'I knew that the Resurrection would be directed
from that hill', and he started on a work which was to occupy him for
many years afterwards, the *Port Glasgow Resurrection*, again writing,
'The discovery of Port Glasgow was a great joy. So much so that I felt
at rest when I came to the Port Glasgow Resurrection'. Even after com-
pleting this painting, Spencer continued to revisit Port Glasgow and paint
there. His *The Glen, Port Glasgow*, from 1952, hangs in Glasgow's
Kelvingrove Art Gallery and Museum.

Port Glasgow Resurrection shows people rising from their graves in
the cemetery, re-uniting with their loved ones and recommencing homely
daily tasks. But those resurrected are dressed in the tweeds and print
frocks of small-town rural England, and bear no resemblance to the
inhabitants of Port Glasgow. As an artist Spencer was no social realist,
still less a socialist realist. His Port Glasgow paintings may be great art,

---

[1] The quotations from Lithgow workers about Stanley Spencer are all taken from
the excellent booklet published by Glasgow Museums in 1994, *Canvassing the
Clyde: Stanley Spencer and the Shipyards*, by A. Patrizio and F. Little.

but they are not great social history. Nevertheless, there should be some way in which these striking compositions could be used a public art to enliven and brighten Port Glasgow. What about covering the 1960s shopping centre with huge reproductions of Spencer's work? Or lining the old shipyard wall on the Greenock Road with Spencer murals?

Port Glasgow awaits its spiritual resurrection, as foreseen by Spencer: on my last visit the dead still appeared to be resting quietly in their graves. Sadly, the town still awaits its earthly rebirth as well, for it remains one of those parts of post-industrial Scotland that social regeneration appears so far to have largely bypassed. Port Glasgow's case may be extreme, but it is not unique. A recent Convention of Scottish Local Authorities (COSLA) report highlighted the problems of small and medium towns in the 'new economy'. The cultural, tourist and financial services type of industries tends to go to the big cities, such as Glasgow and Edinburgh, places which provide a lifestyle infrastructure to support these industries, not to the smaller, post-industrial locations.

The Port Glasgows of the world are not well placed to grab a piece of this economic action. Considerable amounts of its housing stock require millions of pounds of investment in upgrading and little work has come to replace the old industries. (The Playtex factory, manufacturing Wonderbras for the world, is an exception.) The town suffers from large-scale 'hidden' unemployment. Whether or not the new waterfront developments will lead to a meaningful Port Glasgow Resurrection remains to be seen.

CHAPTER II

Greenock:
Escaping the Second Division

NO MAJOR TOWN in Scotland can rival Greenock for its dramatic situation. At 'the tail of the bank', that is the bend on the coastline where the River Clyde turns into the Firth of Clyde, it commands a beautiful arc of panoramic views. From Dumbarton Rock across the river, with Ben Lomond often visible behind, the eyes pan round the range of the mountains of the Cowal peninsula, and from the town's highest points you can look out over the islands of the Firth of Clyde, most notably to the jagged peaks of Arran. Behind Greenock are the heather- and tree-clad Renfrewshire hills, giving the town a backdrop which is a worthy complement to the seascape.

The views to the landward of Greenock's shoreline over the last quarter of a century, however, have not been so pleasant, as the town has undergone painful economic decline, urban decay and severe population loss. From being in the premier league of Scotland's industrial towns through nearly two centuries, Greenock has been relegated. Indeed, the Inverclyde region, to which the town now belongs since local government reorganisation in the 1970s, has the unenviable distinction of being one of the 10 poorest regions in the UK (one of the others is in Liverpool, one is in London, and the remaining seven are all in Glasgow). Greenock also has chronic drug abuse and crime rates, highlighted in the recent Ken Loach film, *Sweet Sixteen*.

But Greenock is a proud town with a significant history, and one which is now showing some welcome signs of a resurgence. Despite being over 20 miles from Glasgow, it is a place I know reasonably well. Often I pass through there to catch the CalMac ferry from Gourock across to Cowal for a day of hillwalking or, if time is limited, I go for a shorter walk on the wonderful Greenock Cut above the town. But Greenock is more than just a place to pass through to get to somewhere else, and it is more often the pleasure of an urban ramble which calls me to the town, sometimes combined with a trip to see Greenock Morton Football Club – but more of that later.

There is a local song about 'The Green Oak that stood upon the square', and the arborial emblem can be seen frequently around Greenock, but the name of the settlement at the tail of the bank has nothing to do with trees; rather, it is derived from the Gaelic *grianaig*, meaning the sunny place. The irony is that, as the song cited above continues:

Now Greenock's no a bonny toon
I've heard some folk complain
For every time they go doon there
There's nothing to see but rain.

Indeed, its rainfall is almost twice that of Glasgow upriver, complicating the work of the urban rambler and photographer.

Greenock does not have a long history, unlike its Renfrewshire neighbour and bitter rival, Paisley. Indeed, it only got its first kirk in 1591. (Paisley, by comparison, has an abbey 900 years old.) Greenock became a burgh in the 1630s, and was at first a fishing port. About this time, Captain William Kidd, the Caribbean pirate, was reputedly born in the town, the son of the local minister. Daniel Defoe visited the place in the 1720s, when it had about 1,000 people, and commented that 'the town is well built and has many rich trading families in it. It is the chief town on the west of Scotland for the herring fishing'. At that time, reports were of almost 1,000 herring boats in the season, most of the herring being exported to France. This industry led to a spin-off in rope-making and boat-building, and in 1711 Scott's shipyard was opened, initially building small craft.

The yard was to become one of the world's greatest and was to be in operation for 277 years, during which time the lower Clyde town (with Port Glasgow) became the greatest shipbuilding centre in the country – after Glasgow. Scott's was not the only, but was always the main, yard in Greenock, and was constantly at the forefront of marine technology. It built passenger ships for the China run, and later huge military vessels, such as the *Ajax* in 1912, of 20,000 tonnes. One of its specialisations was in submarine construction for the Admiralty. It scraped through the depression of the 1930s and for a while boomed on the oil tanker trade, before closing in 1988. When it closed with the loss of the last 2,000 jobs, Greenock's unemployment rate officially reached 25 per cent, though in reality it was much higher than that.

At its height, Greenock's shipbuilding industry employed 7,000 men. Scott's dominated, but there were other yards, such as Cairds, which built many of the Clyde paddle-steamers. Greenock was prosperous: industry was generally male dominated and skilled, unlike in Paisley where it was female dominated and unskilled. Mill lassies in Paisley earned the equivalent of 50p a week; shipyard workers in Greenock more than double, nearer treble, that. Other industries followed shipbuilding. Marine engineering, where the firm of J. G. Kincaid was a world leader, the Clyde Pottery, sail- and rope-making with the Gourock Rope Company, sugar refining with firms like Walkers and Lyle's (later Tate and Lyle with 50 per cent of UK sugar output), and many others. Population growth was rapid. By 1799 the town had 15,000 inhabitants, and further growth made it a parliamentary burgh in 1833.

At this time, visitors uniformly spoke admiringly of the town. William Cobbett passed through in 1832, and wrote of Greenock as a:

> great commercial and fishing town, with a population of 30,000, and a custom house like a palace; the streets are regular, conveniently wide; the houses built of stone and everything wearing the appearance of competence and great solidity.

Population growth continued and at the early part of the 20th century Greenock had about 75,000 people, a level of population it maintained until the 1960s. The last main wave of immigration was actually that of several thousand English people who came to the town in 1909 when the Royal Navy torpedo factory was moved to Greenock from Woolwich, to be close to the submarine production at Scott's shipyard.

Greenock repeatedly made frustrated efforts to annex the neighbouring burghs of Port Glasgow and Gourock, and when amalgamation was finally achieved in the 1970s, as a sop to these satellites, the conglomeration was called Inverclyde. Back then, the total population of the three towns was near 100,000; today it is about 75,000, representing the greatest population loss of anywhere in Scotland in that time, outside of Glasgow. And unlike Glasgow, Greenock is still losing population. Scott's, Kincaid's, Tate and Lyle, the Gourock Rope Company – they have all gone. Greenock was, in fact, largely saved by the arrival of IBM in the 1950s. IBM expanded whilst other industries contracted, and at its peak employed 5,000 people. But it, too, has suffered in the 1990s from international competition, and has had to scale down its operations, largely abandoning computer production and concentrating on call centre and repair work. IBM's famous No Redundancies policy, based on the Japanese model, was a victim of this restructuring.

Greenock can proudly claim one of the causes of this massive growth in industry and population in the 19th century as its own. James Watt was born in the town in 1736 and attended the local grammar school, founded in 1727 – though he later moved to Glasgow. Watt's improvement of the Newcomen engine meant that steam power could be applied to industrial production, replacing water power. It also was applied to sea-borne navigation for the first time; though, ironically, it was in Greenock's neighbouring Port Glasgow that the world's first sea-going ship, the *Comet*, was built in 1812. Another irony was that, though steam was applied early to ships built in Greenock, most of the town's factories remained water powered long after this had been superseded by steam elsewhere.

The reason was that the Greenock Cut, Robert Thom's marvellous feat of engineering dating from the 1820s, which supplied clean water to the town's population, was able to supply water power to the town's works even cheaper than steam power could, until far into the 19th century. In 1839, one textile factory constructed the biggest water wheel in the world, at 180 tonnes and 60 foot in diameter, to utilise this cheap power source, estimated at half of the cost of steam power. Indeed, in the 1970s there were workplaces in the town still driven by water from the Cut, though turbine powered rather than wheel driven.

Another, probably greater, cause of Greenock's expansion was the Union of 1707, which opened England's colonial trade to Scotland. Nowhere was better placed to exploit this than Greenock, which soon replaced Bristol as the main entrepôt for many colonial commodities, including sugar and tobacco, once the town had opened its first harbour in 1710. As the Clyde was not navigable at the time to large vessels, most disembarked their cargoes at Greenock (and Port Glasgow), before they were carried further upriver. Greenock became rich – as well as from her own industries – as Glasgow's middleman. Greenock even had its own sugar exchange and tobacco exchange. Though it did not, unlike

Bristol and Liverpool, become involved in the actual slave trade, it cannot be denied and is worth remembering that much of Greenock's wealth, later diverted to industrialisation in the 19th century, came directly from the misery and exploitation of legions of African slaves in the sugar and tobacco plantations of North America. Slavery, however, is not mentioned in J. L. Dow's book *Greenock*, nor in Greenock's McLean Museum.

Further expansion of the harbour and docks followed – the East India harbour in 1809, the Victoria Dock in 1850 and the James Watt Dock in 1886 – making Greenock (until later eclipsed by Glasgow's widening of the Clyde) Scotland's main port for imports and exports for much of the 19th century. Today, Inverclyde's logo proudly proclaims the area as the export capital of Scotland. On a reduced scale, this may still be true, but ironically, one of Greenock's main exports was always people, and the export of almost one-third of its own population in the last quarter of a century is a sad example of this. In Victorian and Edwardian times, its quays were the main exit points for emigrants to the United States and Canada and to Australia and New Zealand, many of them poverty-stricken refugees from the Highland area. On the other hand, Greenock was also the entry point to Scotland for Irish immigrants, and to those from Eastern Europe. Like Glasgow (but unlike Paisley) it was a cosmopolitan place, with a buzz of nationalities and languages in its streets, or at least on the waterfront and in its railway stations. This was even more so during the Second World War when Greenock became the UK base for the Free French Naval Forces, and the main entry point for US soldiers to the European theatre of war.

My adoptive Glasgow has cropped up a few times already in this meditation on Greenock, and I really do feel when at the tail of the bank that I am simply in a detached part of the Dear Green Place. Elsewhere, I have written that Paisley, Greenock's Renfrewshire rival, is definitely not Glasgow, despite being contiguous with it. With its heavy industrial past in shipbuilding, its cosmopolitan seafaring character, and its long-standing close economic contacts with Glasgow, Greenock paradoxically seems nearer, closer culturally, to Glasgow than Paisley, despite being more than twice the distance away.

The wealth that the human traffic brought to Greenock from international shipping was supplemented by the more modest economic gains of coastal shipping to the Highlands. This was largely monopolised by the town, to a great extent through the firm of MacBrayne's (originally Hutcheson's) which still has its headquarters in neighbouring Gourock. MacBrayne's steamers plied the west coast and islands of Scotland, with passengers and cargoes, and Greenock was also a major port of call for the pleasure steamers which came 'doon the watter' from Glasgow during the Glasgow Fair and at other times. Greenock looked outward to the world, Paisley looked inward to its rural heartland from where most of its population came – hence the difference in local character.

Greenock today

It is about half an hour by train from Glasgow Central to Greenock Central, the starting point for an exploration of the town. We often forget that Watt's invention made possible not only steam-powered factories and water-borne navigation, but also the railway system. The Glasgow, Paisley and Greenock railway reached the town in 1841. Greenock's first station was designed by the architect who also designed Euston Station in London, and a wonderful painting of the station dating from the year of construction by Thomas Carswell shows us what we have lost. This hangs in the town's MacLean Museum.

We drop down the steps of Station Avenue to Cathcart Street, where was situated the town's main hotel, the Tontine, built in 1801 and demolished in 1892 to make way for the main post office, a building which in turn now hosts the James Watt pub. There was a James Watt bar earlier in Greenock, near the engineer's birthplace in William Street. Both birthplace and bar have been demolished. In turn, the Tontine Hotel moved to a former businessman's mansion in the west of the town after 1892.

Going along Cathcart Street the fine Well Park Kirk is on the left, but it is overshadowed, literally, by Greenock Town Hall on the right. This was built in 1886 at a cost of over £100,000, and is crowned by the thin Victoria Tower, rising a massive 250 feet above the building. Outside of Glasgow City Chambers, this must be the finest municipal building in Scotland, and was clearly meant to proclaim the proud self-image of the town to all its incoming seafaring traffic. A fountain from 1879 commemorating Abram Lyle (of the sugar family), who was Provost of Greenock, stands in Cathcart Square beside the building.

This is impressive, but it is just the back of the building. Going down

William Street will take you to the front of the town hall, and at the end of the street there is a fine statue of James Watt himself, on the site of his birthplace. Though events took him elsewhere, Watt did not forget his home town and in his will left £100 to found a scientific library. The building where the statue stands was built in 1907 as the Watt Memorial Engineering School, but it is now Education Department offices. Circumnavigating the building brings you back round to Clyde Square, where there is an interesting statue, *Men of the Clyde* by Malcolm Robertson, dating from 1975 and showing three shipyard workers dragging a ship's propeller.

When I was last there, in front of the sculpture, on a bench, were three young people, who could have been the grandchildren of the men who posed for the sculpture. Clearly jobless, there were having a drink and a chat. I asked if they minded me taking a photograph of the sculpture – 'nae bother'. Not only that, I was interrogated as to my purpose, and then given a list of must-see places, museums to visit, people to contact... how much was I going to write?

'Three thoosand wurds? Tha's no enough aboot Greenock. Folk think there's naething here, think it's a dump, but see the history o the place...'

And they solved a problem for me. A prominent building on Cathcart Square had a huge Glasgow crest on it – not a Greenock one. What had it been? A Clydesdale Bank was their answer, and the Glasgow-based bank had emblazoned its building this way.

I extricated myself by asking directions to the McLean Museum, and avoided being dragged up the Victoria Tower by another young lad who had arrived and claimed he knew the janitor, by pleading an appointment at the museum, and headed up Bank Street. Here and along Shaw Place to the right are the townhouses of the Greenock merchants and manufacturers of the period around 1800, convenient for their business at the docks. But as central Greenock became an overpopulated slum, ravaged by cholera outbreaks, the middle and upper classes moved westward, where I was headed. In their departure, these fine houses on Shaw Place became multiple occupancy dwellings. The view over the Firth of Clyde from here, past the town hall, is staggering.

Just below Shaw Place were the former central Greenock slums of the 19th century, a teeming pestilential place recorded in many old photographs. Here, too, was the original Greenock Prison, which saw interesting events in 1820. Some Paisley weavers had been arrested in the disturbances of the Radical War of 1820. There is an antipathy between Greenock and Paisley but in 1820 class solidarity overrode it. The Port Glasgow Volunteers had escorted the prisoners to the jail, and were attacked by rioters from Greenock as they left the town. The Volunteers turned on the crowd and fired, killing several and wounding others, before fleeing towards Port Glasgow. Here they barricaded themselves against the Greenock mob, a section of whom had meanwhile gone to the jail and freed the Paisley weavers, overpowering their jailers. The old jail was demolished in 1869.

Walking down some steps brings you to Ann Street and on the left, Tobago Street, its name recalling Greenock's North American links. Here, and going along Sir Michael Street to the right, you are in the midst of high-density social housing from the 1930s and 1940s, most of it appearing to be still in good condition, though not really exuding an air of prosperity. Thereafter, crossing the main road and following Kilblane Street past the bus station takes you to George Square, and another collection of fine public buildings, including many, many churches.

A walk to the top of Nelson Street, which runs into the square, and back allows a view of some of these. On the left are the judiciary buildings and several churches, including the former Gaelic Chapel, and at the top of the street is the James Watt College, a 1970s construction. I nearly got a job there in 1974. I was doing quite well in the interview until asked if I would move to Greenock if I got the job. Being young, I told the truth and said no. How might my life have been different had I lied?

Coming down on the opposite side of Nelson Street is a curious cottage-style building, Ardgowan House. Dating from 1893, it was formerly Greenock's Eye Infirmary, established by Anderson Roger, the Port Glasgow shipbuilders. This endowment was possibly because so many of their own workers would suffer eye injuries in their employment. It is now in general NHS use. Back at George Square, Union Street beckons us left.

From here westwards, mid- and late 19th century Greenock built itself towards Gourock. People who do not know the town will be astonished by west Greenock. Outside of Glasgow and Edinburgh there can be no more prestigious example of a grid-planned middle-class residential development in Scotland. It is a surviving demonstration of the wealth of the town at that time, and of the enormous social divisions it contained. I know

GREENOCK CENTRAL STATION, BUILT IN 1841
Built by the architect of Euston Station,
yet the frontage has been wantonly demolished

of nowhere else in Scotland where there is such a sharp and sudden division of a town in social class terms. Unlike Paisley, which basically had one street of upper-class housing in the 19th century at Oakshaw, Greenock clearly had a broad and very rich middle class.

Despite their wealth, Greenock's capitalists appear to have been much less willing to give to charitable purposes than those of Paisley. The Eye Infirmary has been mentioned, and here in Union Street another example is the museum established by the bequest of a Greenock timber merchant, James McLean, in 1876. This is a wonderful place to spend a couple of hours, though this is not enough. I had been here twice to give talks to the Greenock Philosophical Society, an institution dating from the mid-19th century and still going strong, but had never had time to look around the building.

Nowhere in Greenock can we escape the influence of James Watt. James Watt Street lies next the museum and in the McLean Garden lies a former working steam engine – though from a later period than Watt's – one formerly used at the Greenock docks. And inside, the account of the history of Greenock begins with the story of its most famous, and definitely most influential, son. In addition to an informative display of photographs and physical items illustrating Greenock's history, the museum has a small but excellent collection of paintings, many illustrating the history of Greenock. It also has a large collection of stuffed animals from the big game trips of Robert Scott, scion of the shipbuilding dynasty, if you like that kind of thing. Scott gave his much more interesting – and priceless – collection of armour to Kelvingrove Museum in Glasgow, which was a loss to Greenock, which was left with the bears and crocodiles.

I was lucky enough to catch up with Vincent Gillan, a social history researcher in the McLean Museum, and he was able to clear up several issues for me, such as why I could not find the original Greenock Central Station, apart from some parts of the portico: it had been damaged and later demolished, I was told. I asked Vincent if he thought Greenockians were more Glaswegian than the Buddies of Paisley.

'Oh yes, definitely,' Vincent immediately agreed. 'We are much more gallus down here. We've got the full glottal stop. I think it's the influence of the river, connecting you to the wider world.'

One example of this connection of Greenock to the wider world is its strong and surprising Gaelic links. Historically, there is no Lowland

HIGHLANDERS' ACADEMY 1835
Educational provision for the town's huge Gaelic population

town more connected with the Highlands than Greenock. This was noted as far back as the 1650s, when a Cromwellian agent commented on the trade of the Highlanders with Greenock and to their seeking employment there. In 1793, the minister at Greenock asserted in the (Old) *Statistical Account* that:

> One may at times walk from one end of the town to the other, passing many people, without hearing a word of any language but Gaelic.

This may at first seem a wild exaggeration, but later the census of 1851 revealed that 11 per cent of the population of the town were Highland born. By comparison, it was less than five per cent in Glasgow. When, to the 11 per cent one adds their offspring, the culturally Gaelic section of Greenock society must have amounted to almost a quarter in the mid-19th century.

The Highlanders formed a Gaelic chapel in the town as early as 1792, and a Gaelic Free Kirk followed in 1848. The sad shell of the latter lies, with identifying original inscription, in Jamaica Street, just opposite the McLean Museum. They established the Highlander's Academy in 1835, and there was also a Gaelic choir. There appears to have been little animosity towards the Gaels in the town, though a local newspaper in the 1850s suggested they should give up attempts to maintain their language, and all learn English. (Greenock had for a while two daily newspapers in the 19th century; today the *Greenock Telegraph* survives as a twice weekly.)

As well as a place to settle, Greenock was a departure point for emigrant Highlanders, and here we must mention the writer John Galt. Born in Ayrshire, he came to Greenock as a boy, wrote most of his famous works here and eventually died in the town. One of his other business activities was organising emigration through the Canada Company. In Canada, he founded the town of Guelph in Ontario. Many of his clients were Gaels seeking a new life. However, his efforts in this sphere bankrupted him, and he returned to Greenock to his interrupted career of writing for a living. We will bump into Galt again on our pedestrian peregrination.

From the McLean Museum you can head directly back to central Greenock, and then to the waterfront. But another option is to survey the wonders of West Greenock, by following Union Street to Ardgowan

Square, where we can see the relocated Tontine, still a hotel, and then proceed until Union Street becomes Newark Street, heading ever westward, always passing interesting buildings. An example is the Sir Gabriel Woods Mariners' Asylum, established in 1850 by a local boy turned successful diplomat. In his will, he left £8,500 to build this extravagant Tudor-revival rest home. Greenock, sadly, eventually ran out of mariners and in the 1960s this home was converted to an old folks' home. Most of the buildings in west Greenock are of a very high standard architecturally, and the whole area is wonderfully coherent. But I hope I will gain no enemies by saying that there are no exceptional buildings here, none of architectural genius. Greenock had no Mackintosh, or 'Greek' Thomson like Glasgow, or even, dare I say it, no-one to match Tait of Paisley.

It is worth going on as far as the Battery Park, established as a defensive point in the Napoleonic Wars, a connection recalled in the name of the nearby railway station, Fort Matilda. Then you can turn back down Eldon Street, passing the Coastguard Station, which is another reminder of Greenock's still-living links with the sea, and return to central Greenock along the esplanade. If you don't know Greenock, this is a real marvel. There can scarcely be a coastal walk in the whole of the UK to compare with this. On the one side there are successions of fine late Victorian villas, and on the other there is the wondrous scenery of the Firth of Clyde. It is a long walk, and you might want to pause during it at the monument to John Galt erected on the esplanade. If Watt was its most famous native son, Galt was equally the most famous adoptive son of Greenock. He was a social novelist with a fine eye for historical change, and his most important novel, *Annals of the Parish*, chronicles the Industrial Revolution in an Ayrshire town. He also wrote *The Provost* and *The Entail*.

Paisley may have had its poets, the long line of radical rhymesters bred from its hand-loom weavers, but Greenock produced none of those. It has, however, its literary traditions aside from Galt. There is the fact that the town claims to be the home of the world's oldest Burns Club, the 'Mither Club', established in 1801 – though Paisley disputes this. I think the fact the Burns' Highland Mary lies buried in Greenock adds to the town's claim here. In the 1960s the local writer Alan Sharp, later enormously successful as a Hollywood script writer, produced the novel *A Green Tree in Gedde*. Then in the 1970s local playwright Bill

LAUNCH FROM SCOTT'S SHIPYARD, 1818
An early launch from what was to become the world's longest-lasting shipyard

Bryden had success with *Willie Rough*, a play based on his grandfather's shipyard experiences at the time of the Red Clyde, and since then Peter MacDougall has written several plays commenting on the turmoils and hardships of the period of Greenock's industrial decline. And on culture, let us not forget that it was a man from Greenock, the composer Hamish MacCunn, who wrote possibly the only piece of music by a Scottish 19th century composer that is still performed, the hugely popular *Land of the Mountain and the Flood*. You may well hear its strains inside your head as you walk along Greenock's esplanade.

At the end of the esplanade is the (New) Old West Kirk, built in 1928 to replace the original 1591 place of worship. Here we are back into what is left of industrial Greenock, and the Clydeport container base is framed by some imaginative new dockside housing. With the closure of all of Glasgow's docks, what little cargo trade there is on the Clyde is

LAUNCH FROM SCOTT'S SHIPYARD, 1968
In the 1960s the yard employed as many and produced as much tonnage
as it has ever done

once again centred on Greenock, and at the Clydeport facility you can watch what are virtually the only working cranes unloading on the upper river. This area is curiously known as the Bay of Quick, and was a favourite locus for painters in the 19th century because of the impressive view. A right up Campbell Street, a left along Brougham Street under the railway bridge and then Grey Place brings you to West Blackhall Street, where there are many locations for refreshment, though Greenock has not yet quite developed a pavement café culture.

From here, the town hall looms tantalisingly ahead, above flyovers and major road underpasses, and it almost takes skill in orienteering to get back to the civic buildings and the waterfront. There is inadequate signage and no designated pedestrian access routes. I found a group of American tourists, on their half-day's leave from their luxury cruise liner, wandering

CUSTOM HOUSE, 1820s
Cobbett rightly described it as 'a palace'

hopelessly lost in the car park of the Oak Mall shopping centre. One great advantage of Greenock's deep water facilities has been that it is the only Scottish west coast town which can take the giant luxury liners which sail the North Atlantic and the Baltic cruise routes, and this has brought a lot of business. But if towns are ever to become pedestrian and tourist-friendly, the tyranny of the car must be curtailed. And Greenock's road developments and attendant shopping centres have made the centre of the town an extremely difficult place for walkers to get about.

From the front of the town hall the Custom House is, however, signed and accessible, and no-one on a visit to Greenock should miss it. Like the town hall, the view of the Custom House from the back is impressive enough, but the view from the front, with the high-rise flats of Greenock behind looking like pagodas, is quite staggering. As befits what was Scotland's most important customs house for a century, this is, as Cobbet said, 'a palace'. Built in a Classical-revival style in 1818 by William Burn, an Edinburgh architect, the building still retains part of its original functions, and there is also a small but interesting museum inside. Outside, the building is complemented by the attractive Victorian cast-iron fountain and street lamp, the work of local engineering firm

Rankin & Blackmore. More good housing and an annex of the James Watt College complement one side of the Custom House Square.

But the other side! Desperate for any development in the 1980s and 1990s, when it was designated an enterprise zone, Greenock's waterfront attracted the classic aspects of what I call 'Uglification'. There are far too many fast food outlets and amusement centres occupying what is prime development ground, which needs high-class iconic buildings. Hopefully, in the yet undeveloped East India Docks and Victoria Docks which lie further east of here, we will see better quality redevelopments. And redevelopment is coming, if slowly, to a waterfront that looked as dead as a dodo 15 years ago.

Walking eastwards along the curiously named Rue End Street, the next point of interest after the still-empty Victoria Dock is the site on Main Street of the old Cartsburn yard of Scott's shipbuilding company, which closed in 1988. Today, it is as though it had never existed, and sadly there is no commemoration of what was the longest-in-existence shipyard in world history. This was always Greenock's biggest employer, and the Scotts were important people in the town. Like most 19th-century Scottish industrial towns, Greenock was predominantly Liberal in politics – though the Scotts themselves were Conservatives. Liberalism survived much longer in Greenock as a political force than elsewhere in urban Scotland, and the party only lost the parliamentary seat to Labour in 1936 – where it has largely since remained.

The Liberals' survival in Greenock was due partly to the split in the working-class movement between the world wars. Based mainly on the shipyards, the Communist Party was for a while a powerful force locally, and gained representation on the council. In the 1922 General Election, the Communist Party and its candidate A. Geddes came within 750 votes of taking Greenock from the Liberals, and of matching Newbold's achievement for the communists in Motherwell that year. At subsequent parliamentary elections the Communists gained almost as many votes as the Labour party, a split which kept the Liberals in. And the ghost of Liberalism still occasionally walks in Greenock; in the 1970s and then again in the 1990s, they emerged as the major force on the local council.

The workers in the lower Clyde yards were not directly involved in the Upper Clyde Shipbuilders (UCS) campaign of the 1970s to save the Upper Clyde yards, although they provided it with financial support. At

THE *NORDIC CLANSMAN* (1973)
One of the largest ships ever launched on the Clyde. Yet in 15 years
the yard would close for ever

that time, the tanker boom was at its height, and Scott-Lithgow (as it is now named) built probably the biggest ship ever launched in Scotland in 1974, the 260,000-tonne *Nordic Princess*. Scott-Lithgow, with 7,000 workers, was looking for 3,000 more, and the future of the lower Clyde, deep water yards – which were also boosted by the North Sea oil bonanza and resulting oil platform work – seemed as secure as that of those on the upper Clyde appeared hopeless. Ironically, there are still 3,000 shipyard workers employed in Glasgow, and only 300 on the lower Clyde, at Ferguson's of Port Glasgow.

The Scott's Cartburn site has been occupied by a Holiday Inn hotel, and a couple of call centres for the Royal Bank of Scotland and T-Mobile, successful examples of Greenock getting access to the 'new economy'.

Another example of this is the establishment of the BPI polythene recycling plant at the Port Glasgow edge of the town. Up may have been the only way for Greenock to go, but it is going there slowly.

At a roundabout, where we join East Hamilton Street, there is more redevelopment. On the right, the old Kincaid's engine works has been demolished and new, if somewhat uninspired, housing has gone up.

On the riverside of the street lies the enormous complex of the James Watt dock, parts of which is still used for some non-container cargo, whilst others house the dingy dens of third world-type workshops that could probably not survive elsewhere. Here there is some much more imaginative housing – riverside townhouses built in a decorated brick style that complement the river setting. A glance further along the dock and you see their inspiration: the huge, but sadly derelict, 19th-century brick dock warehouses. These are a glorious monument to the industrial era and are on the UNESCO list of 'most in danger' important heritage sites in the world. Like the hammerhead crane which towers over the docks, this warehouse complex is A-listed.

But what to do with it? There have been suggestions for conversion to housing, and also that the James Watt College could move lock stock and barrel into the site. Cost implications appear to have stalled both developments, and the building slowly rots; a slowness speeded by a major fire earlier in 2006. To find out what the word on the street about the warehouses was, I nipped into the Norseman pub across the road. This had been taken over by an old colleague of mine, Stuart MacMillan, a few years ago based on two assumptions. One, that the warehouses would soon house hundreds of thirsty yuppies or even better, students. And two, that Morton Football Club, in the shadow of whose ground the Norseman lies, would regain their 1980s Premier League position, producing thousands of drouthy punters every second Saturday. Stuart was rather phlegmatic about the fact that neither of his dreams for riches had come true, nor does either seem likely to in the near future, in his opinion. Meanwhile, the Norseman remains less a boutique gastro-pub than a hard-drinking concrete pillbox.

The area behind the Norseman, crumbling Cappielow, where Morton Football Club was founded in 1879, almost matches the state of the warehouses, and shows how far Greenock still has to go. Morton struggled unsuccessfully year after year to escape from the second (really the third) division, a mission finally achieved in 2007. After local government reorganisation, Inverclyde Council offered to support the team and build a new stadium, provided it changed its name to Inverclyde FC. Never! Rather die! Morton refused the chance, and since then have aggressively called themselves Greenock Morton, just to avoid any confusion.

Morton have had their glory days rationed since they beat Rangers in the Scottish Cup Final in 1922, but they did scramble into the Premier League in the 1980s, and as an Aberdeen supporter I found myself frequently at Cappielow. At a time when the Dons could beat anybody – including Real Madrid – we could not beat Morton, largely due to the corner and free kick-taking prowess of who the 'Ton fans still regard as their greatest ever player, Andy Ritchie.

But I don't bear grudges, and once or twice a year I come to Cappielow to support the 'Ton. One reason is that the quality of the banter at Cappielow is very high, and though they have a loyal, long-suffering support of 2,500, they are thinly enough spread on the terraces to be able to hear the witticisms. A couple of examples follow.

The 'Ton goalie was having a bad day and let in a third goal. A disgusted supporter threw a pie into the penalty area, and as the goalie emerged from the net with the ball, a seagull swooped down and grabbed the pie from beneath the keeper's feet. 'Thank Goad' muttered a punter on the terracing, seeing the seagull, 'a substitute goalie at last'.

On another occasion, the team was drooping off downcast after a less than inspiring performance, and a desultory clapping went up from a few fans. 'Clap? Clap?' cried an outraged fan. 'Dinnae clap, the hale teams got the **** awready.' The humour is worth the entrance money, even if the football isn't always.

If you head up Sinclair Street from the Norseman, passing Cappielow itself on the right, and go under the railway bridge, a right turn along Carwood Street soon takes you to Cartsdyke Station. On the journey back to Glasgow, you may feel that you have never really left it. And the pals I had made behind the Town House had proved their point. Three-thousand words wasn't enough for Greenock, and even more than double that doesn't come near to doing it justice. Despite the tribulations of the 'Ton, Greenock is Premier League.

CHAPTER 12

Dumbarton:
From Alcluith to Denny's Town

THIRTY YEARS OF POUNDING the pavements has, I hope, earned me my 'street cred' in Glasgow. But when I am walking around, and writing about the various satellite towns surrounding the Dear Green Place, I am aware that some might regard me as an 'ootlander'. In Dumbarton it is different. Here, I feel almost a native – for I lived there in a dim and distant past, though admittedly for only six months.

That was in 1970. Scotland was still mainly a manufacturing nation, and was crying out, in an era of full employment, for skilled workers. Generous schemes were offered to the unskilled to retrain, and guaranteed jobs, often with guaranteed housing allocations, awaited those who undertook courses at government training centres. There was no training centre in Aberdeen, so when I signed up for an engineering skills course, I was told I had to go to Dumbarton. I agreed, though my geography then was vague, and I thought Dumbarton was in Fife, and not on the River Clyde.

I spent six months in Dumbarton and got to know the town well. Denny's Shipyard, which had been the main local employer for over a century, had closed just a few years earlier. But the town was still based on manufacturing: Babcock and Wilcox, Diamond Power, the Dennystown Forge and Hiram Walker's Distillery were big local workplaces, and new industries, such as Polaroid, had moved into the town. I trained to be a miller and grinder, and I got a job immediately on my return to Aberdeen. Are there any millers and grinders left today? Who now would even know what a miller and grinder did?

My own experience was brought forcefully to mind when I was recently at the Denny Ship Tank in Dumbarton. This is a place I visited many times over the years with my history students, and later with my son. When it was opened in 1882 as the brainchild of William Denny III, the tank was at the cutting edge of shipbuilding technology, giving Denny's a huge competitive advantage in improving both ship safety and in the fuel economy of its final designed products. Shipbuilding was a skilled job down in the actual Denny yard itself where the vessels were constructed. But here in the Ship Tank, the work was much more skilled. From the draughtsmen who produced the drawings to the tradesmen who completed the wax moulds of the model ships' hulls, the quality of craftsmanship demanded was of the highest. This one can confirm, and relive, in the hands-on experience offered during a visit to the tank where you can work with the wax in imitation of the model designers, as well as see the tank in operation.

But that is not all. Specialised tools are on display, which were needed for the tank workers; they couldn't use the regular yard tools, but required miniature planes and tiny shaping equipment. One looks at these tools in wonder and thinks that somebody further down the production line made these bespoke tools for the tank's workers. They, too, were skilled to a degree that assuredly no manual worker is today. And they, too, and their skills, have vanished. The Denny Tank, which is A-listed, was the world's first civilian ship model experimentation tank. It is the length of a football pitch (73 metres) and contains 1.75 million litres of water. The tank is now a detached part of the Scottish Maritime Museum. As well as the tank itself, here you can see a fully restored draughtsman's drawing office from the 1920s, and engrossing exhibitions about Dumbarton and its shipbuilding traditions.

The tank was in full-scale operation for 100 years, and was used commercially by Vickers shipbuilders into the later 1980s. They had bought it in 1964 after Denny's shipyard closed down. Thereafter, the tank was utilised by students of naval architecture, mainly from the University of Strathclyde. Sadly, this too has stopped, and now the tank functions as a heritage centre, and a unique and wonderful one it is. It is the only surviving part of the Denny shipyard, which closed its doors in 1963, an early casualty of changing economic circumstances on the Clyde. The shipyard lay between the present ship tank and Dumbarton Rock and Castle, which must have made it the most scenically situated shipyard anywhere. And though the shipyard has gone, the Rock remains, and reminds us that Dumbarton is one of the most ancient settlement sites in Scotland, and indeed, in the UK. Small wonder the locals call themselves (and Dumbarton Football Club takes the nickname) 'The Sons of the Rock'.

DENNY'S SHIPYARD, 1855
'There can hardly have been a works more pleasantly situated.'
Who could disagree?

The Rock and Dumbarton Castle should be the first port of call on a trip to Dumbarton. Elsewhere, I have praised Paisley's fine raised Victorian station at Gilmour Street. The Sons (and Daughters) of the Rock go one better and have two such raised monuments of fretted wood, rows of rivets and cut glass: Dumbarton Central and Dumbarton East. At the latter one should alight, and admire the station buildings before descending to the Glasgow Road. Across the road, at the head of Buchanan Street, is a building calling itself the Dumbarton People's Theatre. It looked boarded up on my recent visit, but a couple of locals assured me it was still in use. I recalled it in a previous existence, when it was proudly known as the Dumbarton Repertory Theatre.

I found Dumbarton to be a fine wee toon, but even by 1970 it was hardly swinging, and I spent most of my evenings in Glasgow. I was delighted as I walked to work one day to see that the local Rep. was putting on a production of *The Caucasian Chalk Circle*, a play by one of my favourite playwrights, Bertold Brecht. This I duly attended. I remember my presence considerably increased the audience, and that, as the Glasgow trains thundered overhead every few minutes, the entire cast would freeze and go dumb until the train rumbled away, when the thespians would resume. It was a dramatic way of keeping the audience in suspense. I'm sure Brecht would have approved of this example of his *Verfremdungseffect*.

One day I must get back up to Bellsmyre, the council estate where I stayed in digs while in Dumbarton. There my landlady introduced me to the Great West of Scotland Diet: bacon and eggs for breakfast, and sausage and chips for tea. My landlord was my first encounter with an example of the self-educated west of Scotland working man, Danny McAfferty, an old Communist Party (CP) militant. A retired shipyard worker, he was still a voracious reader and I had interesting chats with him about his time as a political activist in the 1930s and afterwards. The CP was a force then in Dumbarton, represented at council level. Nationally, for almost 30 years, the town shared its political representation with Clydebank in the Dunbarton burghs, in the form of Davie Kirkwood of the Independent Labour Party. Danny had not a lot of time for Lord Kirkwood, as he became. He did, however, have his blind spots, and was firmly convinced that the Sino–Soviet split was all an invention of the capitalist press.

In between my landlady's two attempts a day to give me a cardiac arrest, I would walk down Buchanan Street to the training centre, which the locals in 1969 still called 'the aircraft factory', after its usage in the Second World War. (The aircraft factory was also a Denny undertaking.) I noted the site is still in industrial use, as Scotia Packaging. Following Castlegreen Street, Castle Road takes us to the foot of the Rock itself. Once all around was Denny's shipyard. On the left, part of the yard was converted into Allied Distillers storage units. Much of the rest of the yard site is derelict and awaiting housing development, although the former fitting-out basin, just below Dumbarton Rock, was filled in and is now the new home of Dumbarton Football Club. The move does not appear to have improved attendances – or results. The last time Dumbarton won a real trophy, the Denny Ship Tank was new.

The twin 240-ft high plugs of the ancient volcano of Dumbarton Rock are majestic in themselves, and staggering when combined with the view west down the Clyde or north to Ben Lomond. Even the notoriously grumpy and difficult-to-please Dr Johnson, who climbed up here with Boswell in 1773, pronounced himself delighted with the prospect. In this he has been followed by countless painters who have made the rock the focal point of their compositions. An example is John's Knox's painting of 1820, *The First Steamboat on the Clyde*, where he juxtaposes the novelty of the *Comet* with the ancient Rock. It has to be admitted that the view is the main attraction, for not a lot remains intact from the long history of the fortified rock. Indeed, most of the extant buildings are Georgian, and, like the commander's house, date from the period when the castle was re-fortified after centuries of decay, against the threat from the Jacobites and later the menace of the French Revolution.

Alcluith, later Dun Breatainn, has a longer history as a fortified site than anywhere else in Scotland or the UK. It is mentioned in a manuscript dating from 730 AD by Bede. It gained the name Dun Breatann from its role as the capital of the ancient kingdom of Strathclyde, which ceased to exist in 1018. Wallace was held here in 1305 before being sent to London for execution. Mary, Queen of Scots gained refuge here as a child before being sent to France. In 1571, at the time of the religious wars, the castle fell to Mary's enemies, led by Thomas Crawford of Jordanhill, dealing a fatal blow to her hopes. Crawford took the castle by ascending the cliff face at night with his men. When repeated in modern times, this ascent was rated 'difficult' by experienced climbers – and they were without the encumbrance of ladders and weapons.

Today, Dumbarton Rock proudly holds the record for having the highest-graded climb for difficulty in the entire world on its rock face. I have never climbed at the castle, but a friend of mine did in the 1960s, when it was discouraged. He found himself arriving at the top of a climb, just in time to prevent a custodian detaching his protective belay, which had been placed around a cannon. 'That'll teach ye,' he was told. 'Ye can pye tae get in like everyboddy else.' I suggest you too pay the impost to visit the A-listed structure, rather than attempting to climb the rock.

It takes about 10 minutes to walk from the castle to the Denny Ship Tank on the junction of Glasgow Road and Castle Street. You will know when you get there, as outside is the engine of the PS *Leven*, designed by James Napier in 1824. As you walk, you could look at the undistinguished shopping centres which have sprouted around here, like a garish, giant flower bed of plastic signage, or you could think of the days when much of this ground was covered by the main enterprise of one of the most innovative shipbuilding firms on the Clyde, that of the Denny family. Their yard opened in 1844 at a time when Dumbarton was still a sleepy wee town of 3,500 people.

There had been boat-building on the Leven since medieval times, but the establishment of the Denny yard put Dumbarton on the shipbuilding map. Aside from the Ship Tank, Denny's had claim to many other notable firsts in maritime engineering, including the first steel-hulled ship and the first all-welded ship. They also completed the famous tea clipper, the *Cutty Sark* in 1869, after another firm went bankrupt building it. The ship is now located at Greenwich – recently it was badly damaged by a fire. But one has to ask why so much of the Clyde's naval heritage is elsewhere: the QE2 as a floating restaurant in America, the *Britannia* in Edinburgh of all places, and the *Cutty Sark* in London? The *Cutty Sark* is so often stated to be the fastest clipper ever built that it behoves me to correct the misconception: the honour belongs to the Aberdeen-built *Thermopylae*, which beat the *Cutty Sark*'s times on the China run. By the time the ship tank opened in the 1880s, Denny's had gone from employing 14 men to over 2,000.

A medium-sized yard, Denny's did not build huge warships or cargo boats, but a diversified range of craft. One of their specialities was steamers, which chugged away as far as the Irrawaddy River in Burma – and on Loch Katrine in the nearby Trossachs. Here the SS *Walter Scott*, built by Denny in 1900, still operates as a pleasure craft. The boat was transported in sections up Loch Lomond by barge to Inversnaid, then overland to Loch Katrine, where it was re-assembled. The Dennys diversified into activities other than shipbuilding, and tried to start, at various times, helicopter production and hovercraft manufacture. This was to no avail, however, and the yard finally closed its doors in 1963. Denny's remained a medium-sized family firm, which by then could not compete in the global shipbuilding market.

Castle Street now leads us towards Dumbarton town centre, always with something of interest to see. Travelling back down Loch Lomondside over the years, my heart would lift on seeing Dumbarton Rock. It would lift further on seeing the huge red-brick tower of Dumbarton Distillery, looming above the ramparts of its red-brick bottling plant, like a Lego castle. The distillery was built in 1938 by Hiram Walker, a Canadian distiller, on the site of a closed shipyard. Hiram Walker claimed it was the largest distillery in the world. It seemed to me to complement the castle. Sadly, the distillery has closed, and most of it is now demolished, though the tower still stands and there is talk of its possible re-development. Adjacent Dumbarton Parish Church, dating from 1811, has fared better, and looks in fine condition. This A-listed building by John Brash sits on a religious site that dates back to the 14th century.

Just past the church, a turning takes you to a pleasant walkway along the banks of the River Leven, which allows fine views across the river to Levengrove Park, as well as back downriver, bobbing with boats, to where the Leven joins the Clyde. There, Dumbarton Castle stands dramatically proud. At the end of the walkway we come to Dumbarton Bridge, which has been remodelled many times since it was built in the 18th century. The bridge takes us over the Leven, and away from former industrial Dumbarton, to where those who made their money from the industry chose to set up their residences on Helenslee Road and Clydeshore Road. This was away from the smoke and squalour, but near enough for commuting convenience. Many built mansions here, including several members of the extended Denny clan.

Helenslee, built in 1866 for Peter Denny, later became Keil School, but has since been subdivided and sold for flats. It can still be admired from the outside, as too can the nearby Levenford House, built in 1853 for Peter Denny. Levenford House has a fascinating history and has been described as the finest house in Dumbarton. The Scots baronial A-listed building had as its architect James Rochead, who built many of Glasgow's West End Victorian terraces. Inside are some excellent stained-glass windows of scenes from Thomas Slezer's *Theatrum Scotiae*, including Dumbarton Castle, and a quite amazing Corinthian-columned fireplace, with carved wooden heads of Scott, Burns, Knox and Buchanan. The building was used for a television dramatisation of *The Prime of Miss Jean Brodie* in the 1970s, and inspired two novels, *The Gothic Chronicles of Gotham* in 1858, where it appeared as Castle Folly, and – probably – A.J. Cronin's 1930s novel, *Hatter's Castle*.

Cronin was (almost) a Dumbarton boy, coming from Cardross, just outside the town. He was a pupil of Dumbarton Academy before qualifying in medicine, and moving from Scotland. His experiences as a doctor in the minefields of South Wales, and his criticism of what he saw as the unethical medical practices of the time, turned him into an early campaigner for the future National Health Service. *Hatter's Castle*, with its depiction of Dumbarton as 'Levenford', made him many enemies in the town. His novels, however, were hugely successful and their sales figures, ensuing film and television adaptations (such as the *Dr Findlay's Casebook* series) made Cronin very rich.

Another (almost) Dumbarton boy was Tobias Smollet, born in Bonhill to the north, and also a novelist, though much less successful than Cronin. Born in 1721, Smollet also attended Dumbarton Academy, and like Cronin left the town early never to return. Smollett spent most of his life in England and wrote picaresque novels, including *Roderick Random* and *Peregrine Pickle*. These had a vogue in his lifetime, but Smollett died in poverty and was largely forgotten. Today his work is being revived and reassessed. Incidentally, Smollett's father, John, was a Commissioner for the Union in 1707 and the Dunbarton burgh's first MP in the British parliament.

But we have digressed from Levenford House. Luckily for the town, Levenford House came into the ownership of the local authority in 1938, and until recently was functioning as the offices of the West Dunbartonshire Library Services. This arrangement allowed the building to be used for the community, and also to be visited on the annual Doors Open Day, when its interiors could be admired, and its history explained. Alas, no more. For a measly sum of £750,000, Levenford House was put on the market, to later be disposed of. A drop in the bucket of local finances has been accepted for the loss of one of the town's most prized assets which, with a bit of imagination, could have become a valued community asset and tourist attraction – a Smollet and Cronin Museum, for example?

A possibly even finer house stood nearby, and is also now gone. This was Bellfield, which had been inhabited by several Dennys until it was remodelled in 1883 and Peter Denny Jr took the lease. In 1914 it was occupied by the manager of the Dennystown Forge, Robert Humble. The owners of the forge, which produced a variety of castings mainly for the shipbuilding industry, achieved a coup when they lured Robert Humble, a manager at the giant Parkhead Forge in Glasgow, to work for them in 1886. One of his sons was Ben Humble, who, despite the early onset of deafness, was to be a world pioneer of forensic dentistry.

Ben Humble also made a great contribution to Scottish mountaineering as a result of his work for mountain safety and through his many mountaineering books, the best of which is probably *The Cuillin of Skye* (1952). There is something about Dumbarton, possibly the visibility of Ben Lomond, that encourages mountaineers. Several of the Denny family, for example, were founding members of the Scottish Mountaineering Club (SMC).

Ben's story has been told by Roy M. Humble in *The Voice of the Hills*. Ben, cited in this book, described Bellfield in glowing terms:

> How I loved that house! It was built round a courtyard, with 16 rooms in all. The grounds were three to four acres with tennis courts at the top of the garden there was a greenhouse with vines, and a conservatory. Upstairs the drawing room ran the whole width of the house, it was said to have the best dance floor in Dumbarton.

Humble described his father, who appeared to be a fish out of water. Despite his enormous work ethic and technical competence, he appeared not to fit with Dumbarton's small, close-knit, upper-middle-class society, spending his time at work and at home with his workmen, who were regular visitors. He was also, Humble noted, an early socialist, and reader of *The Clarion*. His distance from Dumbarton society possibly saved Humble Sr. from involvement in a disastrous scandal which hit the town in the years before the First World War. Again, let us quote Ben himself:

> When I was a young schoolboy I remember seeing the large letters KOSMOID all across the town. A Glasgow doctor with a big practice was associated with a chemist who secretly claimed to have found a process for transmuting base metals into copper and gold. Several wealthy people subscribed to the firm's initial capital. The initials which formed the name of the firm were said to have come from the first letters of the partners' names: K for Lord Kelvin, the two O's for Lord and Lady Overtoun, S for Dr Alexander Shiels the brains behind the scheme, M for a Glasgow businessman George Millar, D for James Denny and I for Lord Inverclyde. A huge factory was constructed in Dumbuck to the north of the town. Shiels' grand scheme envisaged houses for six thousand workers.

Of course, Shiels was a fraud. The scheme collapsed and Shiels himself disappeared, to be reported dead some months later. What is amazing is that so many rich and intelligent people could be taken in by such a scheme, blinded by greed. Lord Kelvin, for example, was on record as stating that transmutation of elements was scientifically impossible, yet he backed the plans.

Dennystown Forge, unlike Kosmoid, continued to prosper and even in the mid 1970s when I began teaching in Clydebank College, we had many apprentices on day-release from there. I remember them telling me that several old men in their seventies and eighties would turn up every morning at starting time and spend part of the day in the workmen's bothy, for the company and the chat. I cannot imagine today's shelf-stackers and call centre operatives having that attachment to their workplaces once they leave. Dennystown Forge was closed and demolished in the later 1980s as the last of Scotland's heavy industries disappeared.

This area of Dumbarton is no longer the domain of the town's plutocracy – for it no longer has one. Indeed, working-class Dumbarton has spread to this side of the river in a series of housing developments dating from the 1970s. Dumbarton was massively congested up to the Second World War, and most of its admittedly poor housing was demolished. There are few of Glasgow's fine tenements in the town, which makes me wonder why the soap opera *River City*, supposed to be set in Glasgow, is filmed here. At any rate, today the Denny clan's ghosts look out from their fine villas to a series of high-rise council flats.

They may not have Glasgow's fine tenements, but the punters have the patter. I was taking a photograph of Levenford House when a local, temporarily expelled from the pub with his fag, chided me.

'Hey, Big Yin, dae ye no want a fotie o' me? Am I too ugly or sumpin?'

He wasn't Hollywood material, but I thought I would be tactful and state that I probably couldn't afford his fees.

'Right 'nuff,' he came back with, 'but come inside and staund me and my agent a pint and I'll see if I can cut ye a deal.'

A shout from the pub indicated that Celtic had scored against Aberdeen, and that killed off any temptation I may have felt to take up his offer.

Back across Bridge Street takes you to Dumbarton's High Street, which is set in a fine curved form. Though it has no gap sites or boarded-up premises, the High Street does have a tatty feel about it, with many of the buildings poorly maintained or badly altered from their original form. An example is Dumbarton's oldest house, the Glencairn Greit Hoose, which dates from 1623 and was the townhouse of the Earls of Glencairn and later Dukes of Argyll. Old photographs show what a mess has been made of this building, and its restoration should be a priority. Not a priority, one suspects, for West Dunbartonshire Council, which has just sold off Levenford House.

Church Street leads northwards, and here we pass on the right what is known as the Old Academy. Originally built as the Burgh Hall and Library by William Leiper in 1865, it later became Dumbarton Academy and subsequently went through various other uses, including police station and offices, and has been subject to two fires in its history. This Gothic Revival building awaits redevelopment. At the top of Church Street, across Glasgow Road, stands the building that took over the Burgh Hall functions in the early 20th century. The Scots Baronial Municipal Buildings are located in the grounds of the medieval collegiate church of St Mary, whose College Bow from the 15th century still stands. And, demonstrating that one is never far from the Dennys in Dumbarton, a statue of Peter Denny is located to the front of the building. As the West Dunbartonshire Council premises are located elsewhere, Dumbarton has the distinction of having, still standing, two former town halls.

Dumbarton Central Station lies just north of the municipal buildings. Its entrance, on Station Road, is difficult to find; indeed, former entrances have been blocked off, and the station is in great need of investment. A large area of the platform was out of bounds for safety reasons on my last visit. However, this is a beauty of a station even in its present state – and the view north to Ben Lomond also helps pass the time while waiting for the train. If Dumbarton is to benefit from the tourist economy of close-by Loch Lomond and its new National Park, the town needs to make its points of access to visitors more attractive.

The effects of industrial decline have not hit Dumbarton as hard as they have done to, for example, Port Glasgow and Greenock across the River Clyde. Dumbarton's population peaked at about 25,000 in 1971, and though it has fallen, it has done only very slightly to 22,000. There are few areas of visible social decay and malaise in Dumbarton, though its satellites such as Alexandria and Renton appear to have struggled more with the effects of social and economic change in the last three decades. Whenever I am there, I feel that Dumbarton remains pretty much the same fine wee toon as that which I first discovered almost 40 years ago.

CHAPTER 13

The Vale:
Turkey Red to Moscow Red

THE RIVER LEVEN FLOWS into the Clyde at Dumbarton just above the castle, after leaving Loch Lomond at Balloch about four miles to the north. From the outskirts of Dumbarton northwards, the area is known as the Vale of Leven, or as is more common, simply 'The Vale'. There is a cycle track from Glasgow to Loch Lomond and the last few miles goes alongside the smooth and swift waters of the Leven, heavily wooded along its banks and with eye-catching views of the hills to the north. Apart from the frequent fishermen and the odd cyclist, it is usually quiet. But a century ago, these few miles were the centre of the feverish activity of the textile dyeing industry which had been drawn here because of the suitability of the soft water of the River Leven for the dyeing process.

But in 1911 all the factories were quiet, although The Vale itself was a ferment of activity and noise, for the mills were idle due to the great United Turkey Red (UTR) conflict. Over 3,000 workers had struck, and the vast majority of them were women. The strike took everyone – employers, the press, socialist activists and probably the workers them-selves – by surprise, for there had never been a real dispute in the industry since it was established at the beginning of the 18th century. As if making up for lost time, the strike created an almost carnival atmosphere in the town: Lenin once said that revolutions are the 'festivals of the oppressed', and so too can strikes be – that in The Vale in 1911 certainly was.

Strike meetings were held in the local Co-operative Halls, whence workers marched in mass pickets, supported by the whole community, to the various works. There was little strike-breaking, but those who tried to cross the picket lines 'were subjected to a lively time by the female strikers, who threw flour and peasmeal at them, and a number were carried to the river and thrown in', according to *The Glasgow Herald*. Marches through The Vale attracted 5,000 people, and one was led by four bands. The women strikers made effigies of the managers and owners of the mills, and ceremonially hung or burned them, and pelted their mansions with clods and stones. They carried banners such as 'Vale of Leven. White Slaves, No Surrender' and 'We Dye to Live'. The more respectable and cautious male workers, who were generally skilled, despaired of keeping these wild women under control. One especially wild woman who turned up was 'a foreign lady named Madame Sorgue'. She was an activist in the continental anarchist movement, who spoke to the strikers to the distress of both the local press and the trades unions.

Despite these unorthodox actions the strike found general support. *The Glasgow Herald*, as well as the local paper the *Lennox Herald*, was sympathetic to the strikers, and the Independent Labour Party newspaper *Forward* carried reports from the workers, describing their dreadful working conditions and pay. The UTR employers sued *Forward* for libel, but when the newspaper produced sheafs of sworn affidavits from the workers, they dropped the case. While the male workers in the mill, in skilled trades, could earn £2 a week, the females were on 10s a week for a 12-hour day. Many suffered awful damage from chemicals, especially from the chrome used in the dying process, and had holes right through their hands and feet.

Over 2,000 female workers joined the Amalgamated Society of Dyers in 1911 in response to management dismissals of workers. They demanded a 55-hour week, weekly (not fortnightly) pay and time-and-a-half for overtime. Management did not reply, and the workers went on strike. Nationwide publicity helped the strikers' case, as did the support they received from the co-operative movement, which was very strong in The Vale, and which extended credit as well as meeting space to the strikers. The strike was successful in gaining union recognition, and also in achieving some of the workers' demands. The docility for which the workers of The Vale had been renowned was largely gone thereafter. The management – and the trades unions – complained bitterly of the difficulty of keeping the female workers under control thenceforth.

Before the strike, The Vale had been renowned as a classic example of an industrial area with paternalistic and authoritarian employers and deferential, docile workers. A Victorian penny-dreadful novel was written by one James Strang entitled *A Lass of the Lennox*, describing the fortunes of a local millworker whose virtues were eventually rewarded by a good marriage. In reality, their wages were so low that the female workers almost universally quit the mills on marriage. From Balloch in the north down through Jamestown and Alexandria (the biggest town with half The Vale's 20,000 people in 1911) to Bonhill and Renton, several dye-works grew up from the later 18th century, owned by the local families of the Orr-Ewings, the Christies, the Gilmours and the Wylies. As there was almost no other industry in The Vale, these families monopolised the local labour market, and by about 1880 employed over 7,000 workers between them. As well as building the mills, they constructed many of the houses that their workers occupied. These five families dominated local politics, the county council, the school boards, the local churches, and also provided the local member of parliament. Dunbartonshire was represented by the Orr-Ewings from 1862 to 1892 and the Wylies from 1895 to 1906, and their family representatives, Alexander and then Alex, were both Conservatives.

Most local employers simply practised this ingrained method of management and control without much thought. However, Alex Wylie was evangelical about paternalism, writing pamphlets and giving speeches at the local Mechanics' Institute, for example, encouraging thrift, hard work and religious observance as the way to betterment of the working classes, who, in his opinion, should avoid all 'erroneous and subversive doctrines'. At this time, Wylie undoubtedly had an audience in the labour aristocracy of skilled workers in the mills who were the backbone of the Mechanics' Institute, the Savings Bank and the Co-operative. His message had little appeal to or direction towards the mass of unskilled female labour, or for the unskilled, often Irish, male labourers who earned about £1 a week. For these people, Wylie's message was different. The Hibernian, he said, 'has been sent amongst us for a better training' – specifically, to eat oatmeal instead of potatoes and thus overcome his congenital laziness.

Victorian paternalism was always based on favourable economic conditions: a local monopoly of the labour market and little economic competition was what allowed the phenomenon to flourish. In the later 19th century the basis of that paternalism began to crumble, in The Vale as elsewhere. From the 1880s, The Vale's near-monopoly of Turkey Red dyeing began to erode. No cloth was made here, it was simply dyed – not always red, though that was the favourite colour in India, the main locus for exports. The development of an Indian Turkey Red industry hit

The Vale hard (just as the development of an Indian jute industry hit Dundee). In addition, the industry had grown lazy in easy trading conditions and did not modernise. Madder, bull's blood and other materials were used for dyes, when Germany was developing a modern, scientific aniline dyestuffs industry. This Britain failed to emulate, leaving the Turkey Red trade dependent on imported, and expensive German dyes. The response in The Vale was the classic one of British capitalism: cut capacity and keep wages down.

Alexander Orr-Ewing had started dyeing at Croftingean works in 1845. He was MP for Dunbartonshire for over 20 years, and died in 1893 worth £1 million in cash and another £1 million in landed and other property. But such fortunes were increasingly difficult to make by the time his works were being run by John Christie as general manager. In 1897, Christie amalgamated three firms in the United Turkey Red Trust, and by the early 20th century most of the dyeworks in The Vale were owned by the UTR. Ironically, Christie was an industrial chemist who had researched aniline dyes, but the UTR either didn't have or didn't provide the capital to go into artificial dyestuffs production, remaining dependent upon German imports. What Christie did do, however, was savagely cut 'excess capacity' and reduce the labour force by over half to 3,000 by 1911 and hold down wages. Paternalism was now too expensive, and the 1911 strike was the consequence.

Other factors had helped to break down paternalism. The old mill-owning families were dying out – or moving out of The Vale and leaving their works to the care of managers from outside. The electorate was expanding, and in 1906 the Liberals won the Dunbartonshire seat, the first time a non-Turkey Red man had held it for half a century. Some new industry came to The Vale, such as the Argyll Motor Works in Alexandria in 1906, which provided alternative skilled and well-paid employment for men, until its collapse in 1913. Trades unions and co-operatives were growing, and a branch of the Independent Labour Party (ILP) was set up. Although the strike of 1911 was a severe blow to the traditional pattern of social relations which were obtained there, no-one could have foretold the revolution in attitudes which was to take place in The Vale during the inter-war years.

The war provided a short-lived boom for the local economy, as the mills worked flat out and the Argyll works was re-opened as a Royal

THE SIMPLE,
SILENT & COMFORTABLE CAR
10, 12, 15,
20 & 30 HP.
MODELS.

"The Flying Fifteen"

ARGYLL MOTORS.

SHAREHOLDERS' MEETING.

VOLUNTARY LIQUIDATION.

An extraordinary meeting of the shareholders of Argyll Motors (Limited) was held yesterday in the Masonic Hall, West Regent Street, Glasgow, to consider and, if thought fit, pass the following resolution:—"That it has been proved to the satisfaction of this meeting that the company cannot, by reason of its liabilities, continue its business, and that it is advisable to wind up the same, and accordingly that the company be wound up voluntarily." There was a large attendance, the hall being almost filled.

Chairman's Explanation.

■ The palatial premises of the Argyll Motor Works Alexandria.

ARGYLL MOTORS LIQUIDATION NOTICE
This palace of industry saw the birth of, and was an early casualty of,
Scotland's motor car industry

Navy torpedo factory. But the latter was closed in 1919 (though it was to re-open again later), and the mills suffered further erosion of their position after the war, with the UTR closing mills through the 1920s and 1930s. All five remaining works were lying idle by 1938. The Vale suffered a social collapse in the 1920s, when high unemployment led to the closure of local clubs such as the Mechanics' Institute. The two local football teams, The Vale of Leven and Renton, both of which had won the Scottish Cup before 1914, were forced to leave the Scottish League in the 1920s. By 1930, unemployment in The Vale was 68 per cent, and the five towns comprising it were a disaster zone.

A local branch of the Communist Party (CP) was set up, and though very active, it never had more than 100 members. But through organisations such as the Unemployed Workers' Movement (that in The Vale had one of the biggest branches in the UK) and its electoral support, the CP had a major impact on Vale politics between the wars. In the local elections of 1922, the CP and Labour Party won control of the council, previously dominated by local businessmen and landowners, and began to give the unemployed greater provision than that which was allowed under statutory guidelines. Though the council was surcharged and eventually had to capitulate, this series of events gave The Vale its reputation as one of the 'Little Moscows' which sprung up between the wars, and which are described in Stuart MacIntyre's excellent book of the same name.

In The Vale, the CP was led by two very effective and charismatic men, Dan O'Hare and Hugh MacIntyre. Both former skilled engineers currently unemployed, they were tireless in organising their fellow unemployed, supporting strikes such as that against wage-cutting in the UTR in 1931 and at the Balloch Silk Company in 1934. But they were most effective at the level of local government. MacIntyre stood for Dunbartonshire in the parliamentary election of 1931 and won almost 3,000 votes, finishing fourth and last. But the fact that almost all of these votes were from The Vale was shown in the local council elections the next year when the same number of people voted communist, and the Communist Party continually outvoted Labour here in the 1930s – and called the political tune. The old order fell for ever in 1935 when six CP, five Labour and three ILP councillors combined to vote in MacIntyre as Chairman of the District Council, replacing the landowner Sir Ian Colquhoun.

The communists in The Vale combined headline-grabbing agitation with practical local politics in a very effective way. Feeling that deference should not only be dead, but should be seen to be buried, they confronted the old order aggressively. At one council meeting Dan O'Hare told Christie, the boss of the UTR, to 'keep your ass on your chair and shut up'. The chairman of the school committee who refused to increase allowances

UNEMPLOYED MARCHERS LEAVING THE VALE ON A HUNGER MARCH IN THE 1930s
The NUWM was heavily influenced by the Communist party,
which dominated Vale politics at this time

for feeding and clothing destitute kids was warned, 'Your day is coming, The Vale boys will get you'. The local council refused to support either the celebrations for the Coronation of 1937 or those around the silver jubilee of George V in 1935. Instead, local CP-ers painted the roadway on the latter occasion with a huge slogan 'King George, £10,000 a week, George King 15/3d'. Though this rabble-rousing generally went down well locally, O'Hare and MacIntyre were also able politicians.

By the mid-1930s, the CP operated a policy of co-operation with the other working-class parties, with each supporting the others' candidates and not competing for votes. Harry Pollitt, the leader of the CP nationally, said that The Vale gave the best example of the United Front in action in the UK. And at the local level, the left-wing administrations were very effective, engaging in a large-scale programme of council house building, with streets being named after Burns, Hardie, Lansbury – and Friedrich Engels. In addition, public works were undertaken to solve the chronic sewage problem in slum areas such as the Burn in Bonhill, for example. The local libraries became stocked with copies of *Labour Leader* and the *Daily Worker*, in place of the *Daily Mail* and *Daily Express*. Indeed, in the 1930s The Vale became known as a 'Little Russia', as it comprised five villages, rather than simply being a 'Little Moscow'. Its Friends of the Soviet Union branch, again one of the biggest in the UK, regularly sent people to Russia, who invariably came back with glowing reports of progress in the Soviet Fatherland. Even with the onset of the Cold War in 1948 the local council could still stage an exhibition in the local library, entitled 'Thirty Years of Progress in the Soviet Union'.

The Vale remained a stronghold of the CP in the three decades after the Second World War, but their council representation steadily declined, and their influence was felt more through the local trades unions in the decades of full employment following 1945. Boring right-wing Labourism triumphed here, as elsewhere on Clydeside. The Turkey Red industry continued to decline and had disappeared completely by the 1960s, but the Argyll works remained in operation as the largest local employer until 1971. It was joined by an influx of newer light industry on local industrial estates and though The Vale could never be described as prosperous, things were much better than they had been between the wars.

An indication of things to come was given when the torpedo factory closed in 1970, with thousands losing their jobs. The works was bought by Plessey for a knock-down price and they retained 1,200 workers for about a year – before announcing they were moving the many millions of pounds worth of machinery to a factory in England, and laying off the remaining workforce. This led to an occupation of the works by the workers for several months, but it was unsuccessful and Plessey got its machinery. Then, of course, the 1980s came to The Vale, and by 1990 4,000 people, over 35 per cent of the workforce, was unemployed. Depopulation occurred here as elsewhere; for example, the town of Renton's population halved by 2001. The Vale has high rates of all the indexes of social deprivation, including that of bad health. Appropriately, the largest local employer is now the Vale of Leven General Hospital.

I have cycled the route from Glasgow to Balloch many times, but had not done so for a few years, and on my recent visit I noticed that most of the old industrial sites on the River Leven, formerly becoming overgrown jumbles of bricks and foliage, have now been cleared for housing developments. Recently, I walked, taking the train to Renton, the southernmost of the five towns. The route to Loch Lomond no longer goes through The Vale, which was bypassed by the A82 in the 1970s, but even for The Vale, Renton is very quiet. A friend of mine from Dumbarton used to say that they put the Renton drunks out of the pubs and laid them on the street, to avoid blocking the pavement, since the street was so quiet. It seems that is still the case today.

Coming out of the station, a right turn takes you to a monument to the novelist Tobias Smollet, who was born herabouts in 1721. Walking south down the main street you reach a right-of-way sign, whence a path leads to the river and the cycle track. Here, only some old walls still standing round a recently cleared site show the location of the Dalquhurn Works, the first of the textile works to be established here in 1715. It was originally a bleachworks, not a dyeworks – this came later. The Leven is tidal to this point, which allowed horse-drawn barges to service the factory, which later had its own railway siding. Walking northwards, it is delightful beside the river. But signs warn you to keep to the path on account of contaminated land, caused when the mills used the ground beside them for dumping arsenic, chrome and other waste. This certainly doesn't seem to have done the flourishing trees and bushes any harm. The bird life in the river also flourishes, and the fishermen assured me that the salmon and sea-trout fishing is excellent.

To avoid the contaminated land, the cycle track cuts the river bends out in this southern part, and the next industrial site, that of the Cordale works, is passed to the left. It has a little more to show, in the form of a brick building, which the locals told me was the former engine-house for the mill. After another delightful meander, a wooded island comes into view and between it and the far side of the bank lies the former lade of the Dillichip mill, now a whisky bond. Just beyond this site you get the first glimpse of Ben Lomond to the north. The mill lassies would have had marvellous views to contemplate on their lunch breaks.

Approaching the outskirts of Alexandria, there is a football stadium, and inquiries of the punters loafing around confirmed that this was indeed the home of the once mighty Vale of Leven Football Club. The pitch looked playable but the corrugated cowshed of a stand and concrete pill-box of a club house suggested a suitable case for a National Lottery funding application here. I conversed with the apparent devotees, who told me there was a big game next week – against Rangers reserves. I complimented them on their team's fine history. They looked a bit puzzled, until one said, 'Oh, aye, they won a cup or somethin' in the 1950s, was it?'

I was greeted with scepticism when I told the group that The Vale had won the Scottish Cup in 1877, 1878 and 1879. Then one said, 'Aye, maybe so, but we wouldnae know. We are jist here fur tae cut the grass.'

Great as The Vale's achievements were, they pale beside those of Renton who won the Scottish Cup in 1885 and 1888, and then challenged the English Cup Winners, West Ham United, to a super-championship, beat them, and afterwards Renton proclaimed themselves the 'Champions of the World'.

Next comes the Bonhill Bridge, which connects the town of that name to Alexandria. Just north of the bridge is the Ferryfield Works, and further ahead, the clearance teams were working on the site of the Dalmonach Works on my visit. Below the bridge was one of the information points on the Turkey Red Heritage Trail, this one, unlike the others, actually readable and unvandalised. It is pointless spending time, money and effort on such informational activities, unless they are well maintained. From the bridge, cut away from the Leven for a while, and follow Bank Street into the town of Alexandria. You soon pass a nice wee former Edwardian Post office, now a dentist's, but then encounter appalling planning blight.

Between here and Main Street is a nightmare. A mini spaghetti junction has been created to allow cars access to the station, and the biggest car park I have seen outside any main city station has been constructed – but for whom? The Vale has low car ownership, and no-one comes here to work. Beyond this is some poor 1970s council housing and a poverty-canyon of shops on Mitchell Way. There is some good new housing – private, housing association and sheltered – in Alexandria, but the rede-veloped town centre is a disaster. I ducked into Sandra's Café for suste-nance. I had just spent the best part of a fiver in Glasgow on a coffee and croissant before getting the train. In Sandra's I got excellent soup, an apple pie and a cup of tea for £2.80. When I queried the bill, as I thought something had been missed out, the serving lass said, 'Oh no, its right enough. We put up the prices last week.'

Fortified, I continued north along Main Street. To the right was the old working-class housing, and now this land is occupied by council housing and gap sites. To the left were the terraces of the petty-bourgeoisie, and further up the hill, the villas of the owners and managers. Alexandria virtually monopolised what middle-class population there was in The Vale. Unlike even Coatbridge, where the Bairds and others constructed some buildings of note, there is little of built merit in Alexandria. Gilmour Street, to the west of Main Street, contains the Ewing-Gilmour Institute from 1881, now the local library, but it is not a building of any quality. Further up the street can be found the Masonic Institute of 1888, which is grander and has some interesting reliefs and carvings. This was originally the female Ewing-Gilmour Institute, erected in 1888 for 'those humble women who live by toil'. Inside, a mural 'treats of the industries and duties of women' in a pastoral frieze, and the building is emblazoned with couthy mottos, such as 'Wark. Bears. Witness. Wha. Does. Weel.'. However hard they 'warked', these women could not do 'weel' on the wages Ewing-Gilmour paid them.

Possibly the most interesting object in central Alexandria is the Smollet Fountain, dedicated to another of that famous local family in 1870. Alexander Smollet was the laird of Bonhill and MP for Dunbartonshire from 1841 to 1859. And, appropriately, the fountain commemorates his work in bringing a clean supply of drinking water to the town. Another interesting fountain stands in Christie Park, a little to the north. This park was donated to the town by Christie in 1909, just two years before the Great Strike. It appears churlish to belittle these benefactions to towns like Alexandria, but they gave small change back to the population from the vast wealth created by the local workers. And we should remember that until the 1890s there were no death duties on wealth, and that income tax was negligible till the 1900s. Charity was cheaper than taxes.

It was not the dyemasters who brought Alexandria its finest building, which is found a little north of Christie Park, but the Argyll Motor Company, which moved here in 1905, and which produced the Argyll motor car and other models. At its height, 60 cars a week were produced, and the claim that it was then the largest car factory in Europe has therefore to be met with some scepticism. Sadly the under-capitalised venture collapsed in less than a decade, to be replaced by the Admiralty torpedo factory thereafter. The office block of the Argyll has justly been described as 'the most extraordinary industrial palace in Scotland', and by one commentator as an example of 'Beaux Arts Baroque'. The outside is adorned with Peterhead granite pillars, an ornamental balcony, sculptured reliefs of workers (clustered round an Argyll car bonnet) holding their working tools and globes of the world, and is topped with a marvellous clock tower and copper dome. Inside the building is equally striking, with a Sicilian marble staircase, Art Nouveau tiled walls and more marble pillars. You have to think that the cost of the office block must have had something to do with the under-capitalisation of the factory. The factory buildings have been demolished and replaced by housing, but the office block was saved and now serves as a large factory retail outlet. As Alexandria's best building, its retention is something to be thankful for.

From the north corner of the factory, a road takes you directly eastwards and back towards the river, passing the site of the Alexandria dyeworks on the right – this was formed from an amalgamation of the Levenford and Croftingea works, and was the last to close in 1960. The large site is now mostly small trading and industrial units, and houses the Loch Lomond Distillery, dating from the 1960s. Back on the cycle track and heading north again, the last of the great dyeworks was situated on the right, the Levenbank works at Jamestown, whose site is now covered with new private housing. From here, the scene gradually changes from the rest of The Vale, as we enter Loch Lomond tourist country. The river now fills up with boats, boatyards and fishing club-houses, until we arrive at Balloch. This latter town was always a stepping stone to Loch Lomond, and not really part of The Vale, having no dyeworks. But the extension of new housing estates from the 1930s onwards has nowadays joined Balloch to The Vale proper. And my recent visit ended here on a pilgrimage to the housing estate of Levendale, built just south of Balloch station in the late 1930s.

I have seen excellent state housing, from many periods in many Scottish towns, including Glasgow itself. But I doubt if ever a housing estate was built with the quality of design, materials and layout, as well as variety of house styles, as Levendale. This is public housing of the highest quality, though much of the housing units have now been sold, and their consequently rocketing prices will sadly have put them out of the reach of the kind of people they were built for originally. I wondered, as I walked down Lansbury Street, past Burns Street and Muir Street, if, in this housing scheme, a lasting monument to the political activists of the 1930s, the most contentious of the street names still survived. But there it was: Engels Street. And what a great view it lends of Ben Lomond.

Conclusion

Riverrun

OUR RIVER HAS RUN to the sea. At Greenock the Clyde flows into the Firth of Clyde, and then to the wide Atlantic Ocean and the waters of the world. The two centuries and more we have described encompass a world which no longer exists, or does so only fragmentarily and in memory. The Clyde is no longer the greatest industrial river in the world. Most of the industry is gone, and with it the brutality, the exploitation and the misery that was so inflicted on its wage slaves. But so too gone is the antithesis of all that, which was created by working people; not only the political life of unions, co-ops and parties, but also the social life of entertainment and self-improvement which was generated in difficult circumstances and times.

Though the working-class movement failed in its ultimate aim of replacing capitalism with socialism, it was successful in altering capitalism beyond recognition from what existed for most of the period we covered. In many ways the victim of its own success, the labour movement achieved reforms within capitalism, and improved working conditions – but to the point where, in the UK, the ruling classes no longer thought the British and Scottish workers worth exploiting. In the last 30 years, their policy has been – and in this sense North Sea oil was a godsend – to live off service industries, of which the UK has the world's lion's share, and to switch manufacturing overseas to other areas.

The working class, the wage-earning class, still exists, but it has been fragmented and is no longer a social force in countries like the UK. There has been a traumatic restructuring of the working class, where some sectors now enjoy an imitation of a middle-class lifestyle, others are working in low-paid, unproductive jobs, and a huge part of what Marx would have called the proletariat is now expendable and lives outwith economic activity, as the socially excluded, the 40 per cent of the population who don't vote.

Meanwhile, however, the conditions we have described in this book have been reproduced elsewhere in the world, and upon these the prosperity of modern capitalism is – precariously – based. The appalling exploitation of child and female labour, the dreadful housing conditions and the ill health experienced in Scotland and elsewhere have simply been exported beyond the horizon. Women in Bangladesh work in textiles for 4p an hour, as they did in Paisley a century ago, and in Brazil the poor live in favelas reminiscent of the Gartsherrie Rows.

Our parasitic economy of oil and services is dependent on the exploitation of labour elsewhere. It is unlikely that those in China, India, Brazil and other 'emerging' countries will be satisfied for ever with the social conditions they are now enduring, and the consequences of this for the rest of us will be profound. Nor is it likely that in these economies they will long be content to allow the older Western nations to monopolise services such as banking, insurance and advertising. And North Sea oil, unlike whisky, will not last.

Events of recent occurrance have shown the unviability of an economy based on financial and property speculation, and we face recession, unemployment and severe cuts in social services in the years to come.

Our river has run to the seas of the world, but its waters may return in forms yet to be appreciated.

Some other books published by **LUATH** PRESS

This City Now: Glasgow and its working class past

Ian R. Mitchell
ISBN 1 84282 082 6 PBK £12.99

This City Now sets out to retrieve the hidden architectural, cultural and historical riches of some of Glasgow's working-class districts. Many who enjoy the fruits of Glasgow's recent gentrification will be surprised and delighted by the gems which Ian Mitchell has uncovered beyond the usual haunts.

An enthusiastic walker and historian, Mitchell invites us to recapture the social and political history of the working-class in Glasgow, by taking us on a journey from Partick to Rutherglen, and Clydebank to Pollokshaws, revealing the buildings which go unnoticed every day yet are worthy of so much more attention.

Once read and inspired, you will never be able to walk through Glasgow in the same way again.

...both visitors and locals can gain instruction and pleasure from this fine volume...Mitchell is a knowledgable, witty and affable guide through the streets of the city...
GREEN LEFT WEEKLY

Mountain Days & Bothy Nights

Dave Brown & Ian R. Mitchell
ISBN 1 906307 83 0 PBK £7.50

'One thing we'll pit intae it is that there's mair tae it than trudging up and doon daft wet hills.'

This classic 'bothy book' celebrates everything there is to hillwalking; the people who do it, the stories they tell and the places they sleep. Where bothies came from, the legendary walkers, the mountain craftsmen and the Goretex and gaiters brigade – and the best and the worst of the dosses, howffs and bothies of the Scottish hills.

On its 21st anniversary, the book that tried to show the camaraderie and buccaneering spirit of Scottish hillwalking in the early days has now become part of the legends of the hills. Still likely to inspire you to get out there with a sleeping bag and a hipflask, this new edition brings a bit of mountaineering history to the modern Munro bagger. The climbers dossing down under the corries of Lochnagar may have changed in dress, politics and equipment, but the mountains and the stories are timeless.

Dave Brown and Ian R. Mitchell won the Boardman Tasker Prize for Mountain Literature in 1991 for *A View from the Ridge*, the sequel to *Mountain Days & Bothy Nights*.

Walking Through Scotland's History: Two thousand years on foot

Ian R. Mitchell
ISBN 1 905222 44 0 PBK £7.99

Today, walking is many things for many people – a leisure activity, a weekend pursuit, or even a chore – but rarely is it an integral part of everyday life. This book explores the world, and the way of life, that Scotland has left behind.

From the Roman legions marching into Caledonia, to the 20th century's travelling communities, Ian R. Mitchell takes up on a tour of the missionaries, mapmakers and military leaders who have trodden Scottish paths over the last 2,000 years. He also examines the lives of the drovers, distillers, fishwives and workers for whom walking was a means of survival.

This new edition includes a variety of suggested walks and places to visit for each chapter, as an incentive for those who wish to follow in the footsteps of history.

A View from the Ridge

Dave Brown and Ian R. Mitchell
ISBN 1 905222 45 9 PBK £7.50

Winner of the Boardman-Tasker Prize for Mountain Literature

To some, hillwalking is a physical activity. To others, climbing is all, and everything else is nothing. Because it's not just hills: it's people, characters, fun and tragedy. Every mountaineer will know that it's not just about the anticipation of what hill to climb next, it's a subculture of adventure and friendship – all-night card games, monumental hangovers, storytelling, singing – and above all, free spirits.

In this fitting sequel and essential companion to the classic *Mountain Days and Bothy Nights,* Dave Brown and Ian R. Mitchell capture perfectly the inexplicable desire which brings Scottish hillwalkers back to the mist, mud and midgies every weekend. Their lively, humorous and enthusiastic narrative will revitalise the drive in you to get out on the hills – or you may prefer just to curl up on the couch with this book and a wee dram for company.

If you buy only one mountain book this year make it this 'view from the ridge' and savour its rich, different and fascinating reflections.
Kevin Borman, HIGH MOUNTAIN MAGAZINE

Scotland's Mountains before the Mountaineers

Ian R. Mitchell

ISBN 0 946487 39 1 PBK £9.99

Ian Mitchell tells the story of explorations and ascents in the Scottish Highlands in the days before mountaineering became a popular sport – when Jacobites, bandits, poachers and illicit distillers traditionally used the mountain as sanctuary.

- Who were the first people to 'conquer' Scotland's mountains, and why did they do it?

- Which clergyman climbed all the Cairngorm 4,000-ers nearly two centuries ago?

- How many Munros did Bonnie Prince Charlie bag?

- Which bandit and sheep rustler hid in the mountains while his wife saw off the sheriff officers with a shotgun?

- Who was the murderous clansman who gave his name to Beinn Fhionnlaidh?

On the Trail of Queen Victoria in the Highlands

Ian R. Mitchell

ISBN 0 946487 79 0 PBK £7.99

- How many Munros did Queen Victoria bag?

- What 'essential services' did John Brown perform for Victoria? (and why was Albert always tired?)

- How many horses (to the nearest hundred) were needed to undertake a Royal Tour?

What happens when you send a Marxist on the tracks of Queen Victoria in the Highlands? – You get a book somewhat more interesting than the usual run of the mill royalist biographies!

Ian R. Mitchell took up the challenge of attempting to write with critical empathy on the peregrinations of Vikki Regina in the Highlands, and about her residence at Balmoral, through which a neo-feudal fairyland was created on Upper Deeside. The expeditions, social rituals and iconography of that world are explored and exploded from within, in what Mitchell terms a Bolshevisation of Balmorality. He follows in Victoria's footsteps throughout the Cairngorms and beyond, to the further reaches of the Highlands. On this journey, a grudging respect and even affection for Vikki ('the best of the bunch') emerges.

Details of these and other books published by Luath Press can be found at:

www.luath.co.uk

Luath Press Limited

committed to publishing well written books worth reading

LUATH PRESS takes its name from Robert Burns, whose little collie Luath (*Gael.*, swift or nimble) tripped up Jean Armour at a wedding and gave him the chance to speak to the woman who was to be his wife and the abiding love of his life. Burns called one of 'The Twa Dogs' Luath after Cuchullin's hunting dog in Ossian's *Fingal*. Luath Press was established in 1981 in the heart of Burns country, and is now based a few steps up the road from Burns' first lodgings on Edinburgh's Royal Mile.

Luath offers you distinctive writing with a hint of unexpected pleasures.

Most bookshops in the UK, the US, Canada, Australia, New Zealand and parts of Europe either carry our books in stock or can order them for you. To order direct from us, please send a £sterling cheque, postal order, international money order or your credit card details (number, address of cardholder and expiry date) to us at the address below. Please add post and packing as follows: UK – £1.00 per delivery address; overseas surface mail – £2.50 per delivery address; overseas airmail – £3.50 for the first book to each delivery address, plus £1.00 for each additional book by airmail to the same address. If your order is a gift, we will happily enclose your card or message at no extra charge.

ILLUSTRATION: IAN KELLAS

Luath Press Limited
543/2 Castlehill
The Royal Mile
Edinburgh EH1 2ND
Scotland

Telephone: 0131 225 4326 (24 hours)
Fax: 0131 225 4324
email: sales@luath.co.uk
Website: www.luath.co.uk